DIY KIDS'

Dress Up

36 simple sewn accessories for creative play

JESSICA NEAR

www.sewandso.co.uk

CONTENTS

Welcome to DIY Kids' Dress Up where you will learn to make masks, tails, paws and wings to create dynamic costumes for your children to use for everyday imaginary play.

One of the key focuses of my felt creature costumes is to help children learn about animals through play. I particularly want to highlight some of the characteristics that certain creatures are renowned for, and I hope that my costume designs will inspire children to explore the fun that can be had when they dress up and take on an animal's traits.

Dressing up is an important type of play that every child needs to experience. Through dress up and dramatic role-play, children explore the lives of others by imitating their actions, feelings and words. This type of play fosters imagination, strengthens relationships and improves communication skills. Children can practice social interactions in a non-threatening or stressful way if they are behind a mask. Dress up play is a perfect way to help children learn to problem solve, cooperate, and negotiate. While taking on different characters, children can experiment with everything, from voices to characteristics they might not feel comfortable trying in their everyday life.

In this book, you will learn to work with felt, which being a very versatile and durable material is perfect for dress up play. When purchasing materials, look out for high quality felt that is thick, soft and able to handle plenty of tough use. Wool-mix felt will be much more attractive for your projects than lower quality craft felt and will hold up to lots of play. One of the reasons I work with felt is that it is so forgiving. It holds its shape, doesn't need hemming, and allows you to play with many different forms and patterns that you can't achieve with other basic fabrics.

When you've had a go at making a few of the costumes in this book, why not develop your own ideas for different creatures or characters? Perhaps a child you know would love to be a porcupine, or an eagle! Once you understand the basics of working with felt in this way, you can try anything. Go on! Borrow a child's imagination and go on an adventure!

TOOLS AND MATERIALS

FELT

There are several types of felt you can use for your projects. Most craft stores sell felt sheets that come in many colors and printed patterns. This is the cheapest and lowest quality felt, and while the fun prints may be tempting, I don't recommend it as your project will not hold up after even a little play! You can also find Eco-felt by the yard (meter) at most craft stores. It is made from recycled plastic bottles and is affordable, reasonably thick, of good quality, and comes in a wide range of colors. The next level is wool-blend felt. Some craft stores carry this type of high quality felt, but you may have to purchase it online (see Suppliers). This is my favorite type of felt to work with because it is soft but very durable and the range of colors is really impressive.

STUFFING

Polyester fiberfill stuffing is non-allergenic, soft, and easy to use without clumping. This is what I use in all my projects.

SCISSORS

When cutting felt from a bolt or cutting larger pieces down to size, I like to use a rotary cutter or large fabric scissors. If I am cutting out a pattern or trimming my masks after sewing, I use Gingher craft scissors (see Suppliers). They are small and sharp enough to cut small details into thick felt. I keep my scissors in good working condition by sharpening them with a sharpening stone.

NEEDLES & THREAD

I use a universal needle in my sewing machine when I work with felt. The ideal thread choice is 100% polyester. There is no need to match the color of your felt – I use white thread for all the projects in this book.

ELASTIC

For masks I use $3/8$in (1cm) braided elastic in either black or white. You can also find thinner elastic in a range of colors. For tails I use 1in (2.5cm) braided elastic which allows plenty of stretch for all sizes. If you would rather use ribbon, I recommend grosgrain ribbon because it will stay tied, rather than slipping like satin might.

SEWING MACHINE

You do not need a special sewing machine to sew felt. I feel strongly that you should love your sewing machine and feel completely comfortable using it for any project you hope to tackle. I absolutely adore my sewing machine! It is a Bernina that I have been using for about five years now. I have invested in some major repairs, but I don't mind because this machine has worked very hard for me over the years!

TIPS, TECHNIQUES & TRADE SECRETS

★ Your completed felt projects can be spot cleaned or hand-washed in cold water with a mild soap. Lay flat or hang to dry. Washing and drying in a machine is not recommended!

⚡ After a while you may find the felt develops lumps on the surface, known as 'pills'. To de-pill you can use a razor to 'shave' them off. Please keep in mind, de-pilling may thin the felt.

★ These projects are recommended for use by children who are three years old and above. Masks that are designed to fit over the nose and mouth should be reserved for older children. Some children enjoy wearing the masks on their heads, as a 'hat' or headband rather than over their face. Please use caution when giving masks and tails to young children.

⚡ When placing elastic in your masks, be sure it is not twisted. Start sewing where one side of the elastic is secured in place. Once you reach the opposite side, straighten and place the other end of the elastic in the desired spot before sewing over. When sewing the elastic into your tails, be sure it is firmly placed into the end of the tail so that it is securely attached when you sew over the opening.

★ When sewing the hook and loop fastening tape on the armbands, strips should be paired so that a 'hook' strip attaches to a 'loop' strip. Your 'hook' strip should be firmly placed into the end of one side of the armband so that it is securely attached when you sew over that opening. Be sure there is enough left outside of the end so it will attach to the soft 'loop' strip of the hook and loop fastening tape, which should be sewn to the other end of the armband, on the inside. Fold your armband to judge where you need to place this second strip. Hold, pin or glue in place and sew around the outside to secure.

⚡ I recommend gluing your pieces (rather than pinning) for these projects. Many pieces are too small to pin or will move slightly when sewing. When gluing, be careful to use only tiny dabs of glue (just enough to keep the piece in place) and let it dry completely before sewing! If you sew over wet glue, it will bleed through the felt. Or you can opt not to sew at all, and ONLY glue your pieces down.

★ I pin my paper templates to the felt when cutting. This will keep the template in place and allow you to focus on the little details. However, I don't always pin the tiny pieces – I just hold and cut them out carefully, but you can use your own judgment.

⚡ To cut the eyes from the felt, cut a little hole into the middle of the eye then work your way slowly and carefully to the edges. Remember that you can always trim a bit more once your mask is complete.

★ Be sure you get the stuffing into all the nooks and crannies so your tail or paw holds its shape. You can use a stuffing stick to help get into the awkward tips. Try to keep your stuffing light and fluffy as it can easily get clumpy if you are trying to pack it in too tightly.

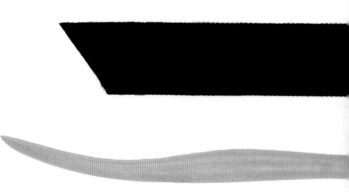

SUPERHEROES

CAPTAIN COURAGE

Superheroes are often portrayed as mythical beings from faraway universes who wield super powers of lightning speed and superhuman physical strength… but everyday superheroes are so much more than fancy weapons and unbelievable abilities. Captain Courage is a real-life superhero who represents every boy and girl who has stood up to a bully, given a friend a helping hand, or simply faced a fear!

You will need

- Two 8¼ x 5⁷⁄₈in (21 x 15cm) pieces of turquoise felt for the mask

- One 3 x 3in (7.5 x 7.5cm) piece of orange felt for the mask circle

- One 2 x 2¹⁄₈in (5 x 5.5cm) piece of yellow felt for the mask bolt

- One 13in (33cm) length of ³⁄₈in (1cm) wide black elastic

1. Copy the superhero mask (see Templates), mask circle and mask bolt templates onto paper and cut out.

2. Cut the ears from the mask template and pin the paper templates onto felt in your chosen colors **(a)**. Cut one mask piece from turquoise felt (including the eye holes), one circle piece from orange felt and one bolt piece from yellow felt.

a

3. Glue or pin the felt circle to the mask and sew in place **(b)**.

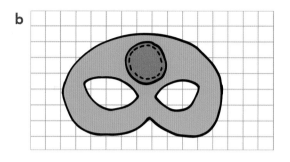

4. Glue or pin the bolt to the center of the circle on the mask and sew in place **(c)**.

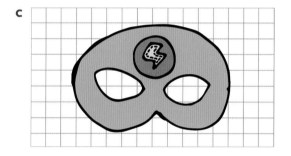

5. Place the felt superhero mask onto a piece of turquoise felt that is slightly larger than the mask and pin the two layers together with the elastic in place on one side of the mask (marked by an 'X'), between the layers. Sew around the edges of the mask to attach the two pieces of felt together. Ensure that your elastic is not twisted as you slide the other end of it in between the layers when you get to that point on the mask, as shown by the other 'X' **(d)**.

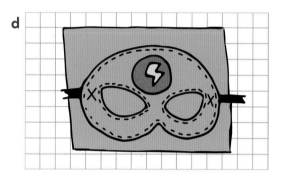

6. Trim away any excess felt around the mask and inside the eye holes **(e)**.

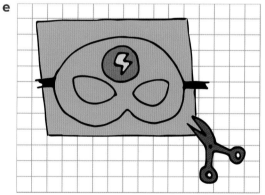

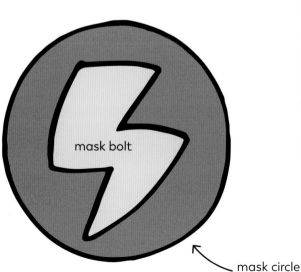

mask bolt

mask circle

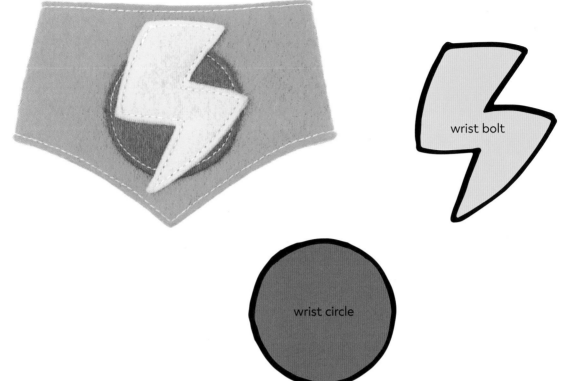

wrist bolt

wrist circle

You will need

- Four 8¼ x 3½in (21 x 9cm) pieces of turquoise felt for the armbands

- Two 2 x 2in (5 x 5cm) pieces of orange felt for the wrist circles

- Two 2⅛ x 1¾in (5.5 x 4.5cm) pieces of yellow felt for the wrist bolts

- Four 1⅜in (3.5cm) strips of ¾in (2cm) wide black hook and loop fastening tape

1. Copy the armband (see Templates), wrist circle and wrist bolt templates onto paper and cut out.

2. Pin the paper templates onto felt in your chosen colors **(a)**. Cut two armband pieces from turquoise felt, two wrist circle pieces from orange felt and two wrist bolt pieces from yellow felt.

a

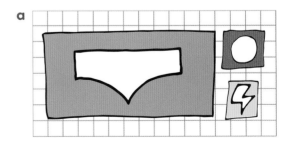

3. Glue or pin a felt circle in position on one armband and sew in place **(b)**.

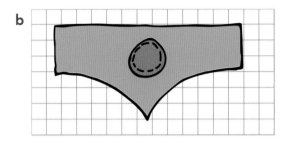

b

4. Glue or pin a bolt piece in position on the armband and sew in place **(c)**.

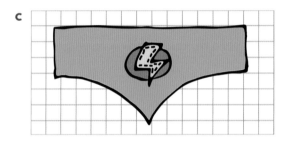

c

5. Place the felt armband onto a piece of turquoise felt that is slightly larger than the armband itself and pin in place. Place one of the hook and loop fastening strips between the two layers of felt on one side, leaving some of the width sticking out from the armband. Sew around the edges of the armband **(d)**.

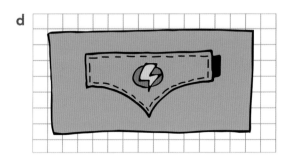

d

6. Trim away any excess felt around the edges of the armband **(e)**.

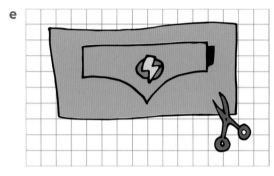

e

7. With the front of the armband facing downwards, place the opposite piece of hook and loop fastening on the reverse side of the armband and sew in place as shown **(f)**.

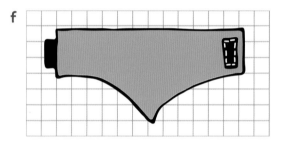

f

8. Repeat steps 3–7 to create a second armband.

LIGHTNING BOLT

- One 14½ x 6¾in (37 x 17cm) piece of turquoise felt for the tail back
- One 13⅞ x 5⅞in (35 x 15cm) piece of orange felt for the tail
- One 11½ x 4¾in (29 x 12cm) piece of yellow felt for the lightning bolt
- One 19¾in (50cm) length of 1in (2.5cm) wide black elastic
- Polyester fiberfill stuffing

1. Copy the tail and lightning bolt (see Templates) onto paper and cut out.

2. Pin the paper templates onto felt in your chosen colors **(a)**. Cut one tail piece from orange felt and one lightning bolt piece from yellow felt.

Try creating other superheroes: swap the flash on Captain Courage's costume for an eco-warrior rainbow and save the planet!

a

3. Glue or pin the bolt piece in position on the tail and sew in place **(b)**. If gluing, only use a very small amount of glue and wait for it to dry completely before sewing.

5. Trim away any excess felt around the edges of the tail without trimming around the opening, leaving a 6mm (¼in) border around the edges as shown **(d)**.

b

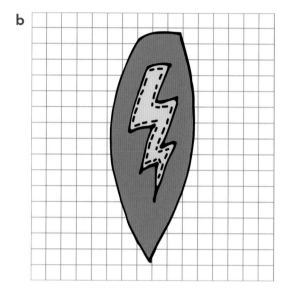

d

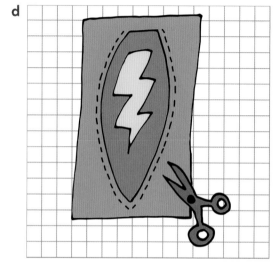

4. Place the felt lightning bolt tail onto a piece of turquoise felt that is slightly larger than the tail itself and pin in place. Sew around the edges of the tail, leaving the straight end open **(c)**.

6. Lightly stuff the tail. Turn the tail on its side, pinch the opening and insert both ends of the elastic. Pin in place and sew across the opening to secure in place **(e)**.

e

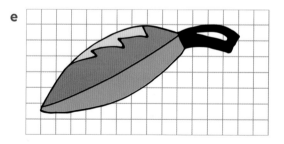

c

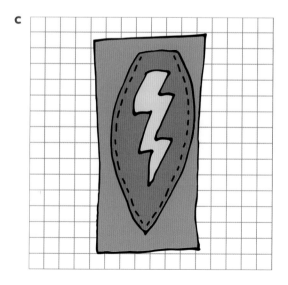

SUPER COMET

Travel the galaxy as Super Comet! Comets are small
collections of dust and ice that whizz in an orbit around a
star. They can be seen in our solar system when their path
takes them closer to the sun and the ice warms up, giving
off gases which produce a stunning comet trail of light.
A light streaking across the sky was often interpreted as
an omen of important, even chaotic, events to come.
Something small, moving at high speed and bringing a
whirlwind of activity... remind you of anyone you know?

You will need

- Two 8⅝ x 5⅞in (22 x 15cm) pieces of purple felt for the mask

- One 3 x 3in (7.5 x 7.5cm) piece of turquoise felt for the mask circle

- One 2 x 2in (5 x 5cm) piece and two 1⅜ x 1⅜in (3.5 x 3.5cm) pieces of yellow felt for the large and small stars

- One 13in (33cm) length of ⅜in (1cm) wide black elastic

1. Copy the superhero mask (see Templates), mask circle, large star and small star templates onto paper and cut out.

2. Pin the paper templates onto felt in your chosen colors **(a)**. Cut one mask piece from purple felt (including the eye holes), one mask circle piece from turquoise felt, and one large star and two small stars from yellow felt.

a

3. Glue or pin the felt circle to the mask and sew in place **(b)**. If gluing pieces into place, use only a small amount and wait until it is completely dry before sewing.

4. Glue or pin the large star to the center of the circle on the mask, and the small stars on the ears, and sew in place **(c)**.

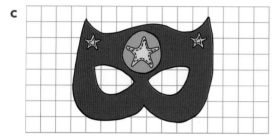

5. Place the felt superhero mask onto a piece of purple felt that is slightly larger than the mask and pin the two layers together with the elastic in place on one side of the mask (marked by an 'X'), between the layers. Sew around the edges of the mask to attach the two pieces of felt together. Ensure that your elastic is not twisted as you slide the other end of it in between the layers when you get to that point on the mask, as shown by the other 'X' **(d)**.

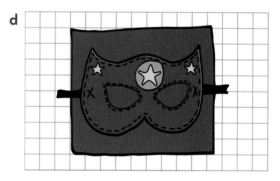

6. Trim away any excess felt around the mask and inside the eye holes **(e)**.

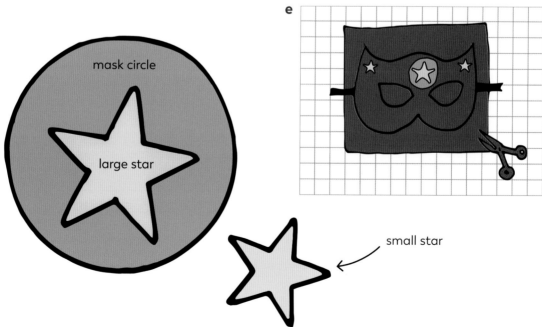

mask circle

large star

small star

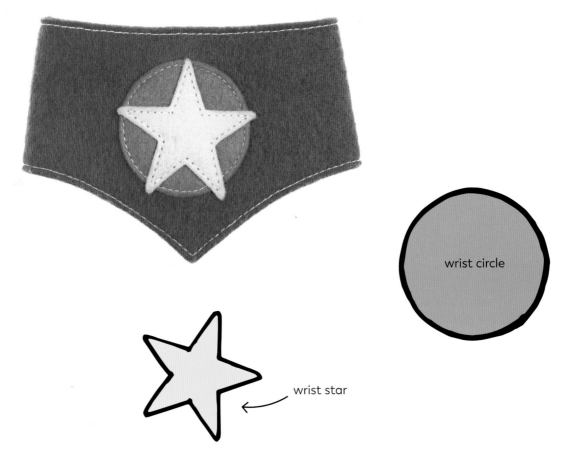

wrist circle

wrist star

You will need

- Four 8¼ x 3½in (21 x 9cm) pieces of purple felt for the armbands
- Two 2 x 2in (5 x 5cm) pieces of turquoise felt for the wrist circles
- Two 2 x 2in (5 x 5cm) pieces of yellow felt for the wrist stars
- Four 1⅜in (3.5cm) strips of ¾in (2cm) wide black hook and loop fastening tape

1. Copy the armband (see Templates), wrist circle and wrist star templates onto paper and cut out.

2. Pin the paper templates onto felt in your chosen colors **(a)**. Cut two armband pieces from purple felt, two wrist circle pieces from turquoise felt and two wrist star pieces from yellow felt.

a

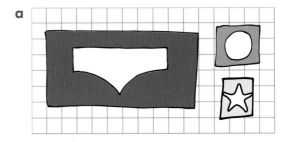

3. Glue or pin a felt circle in position on one armband and sew in place **(b)**.

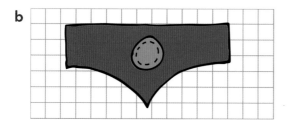

4. Glue or pin a star piece in position on the armband and sew in place **(c)**.

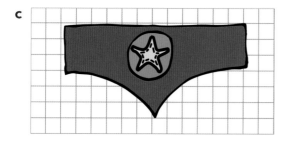

5. Place the felt armband onto a piece of purple felt that is slightly larger than the armband itself and pin in place. Place one of the hook and loop fastening strips between the two layers of felt on one side, leaving some of the width sticking out from the armband. Sew around the edges of the armband **(d)**.

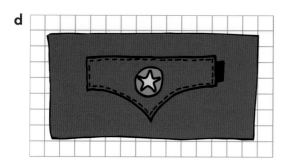

6. Trim away any excess felt around the edges of the armband **(e)**.

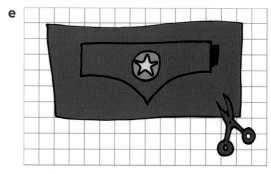

7. With the front of the armband facing downwards, place the opposite piece of hook and loop fastening on the reverse side of the armband and sew in place as shown **(f)**.

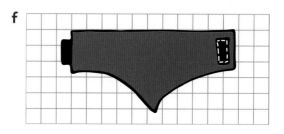

8. Repeat steps 3–7 to create a second armband.

You will need

- One 14¹⁄₂ x 6³⁄₄in (37 x 17cm) piece and three 3 x 3in (7.5 x 7.5cm) pieces of turquoise felt for the tail back and tail circles

- One 13⁷⁄₈ x 5⁷⁄₈in (35 x 15cm) piece of purple felt for the tail

- Three 2 x 2in (5 x 5cm) pieces of yellow felt for the tail stars

- One 19³⁄₄in (50cm) length of 1in (2.5cm) wide black elastic

- Polyester fiberfill stuffing

tail star

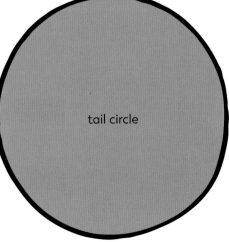

tail circle

1. Copy the tail (see Templates) and tail circle and tail star templates onto paper and cut them out.

2. Pin the paper templates onto felt in your chosen colors **(a)**. Cut one tail piece from purple felt, three circle pieces from turquoise felt and three star pieces from yellow felt.

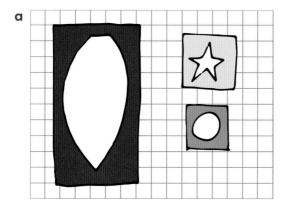

a

3. Glue or pin the circle pieces in position on the tail to form the comet trail and sew in place, then add the three stars in the same way and sew in place **(b)**. If gluing, only use a very small amount of glue and wait for it to dry completely before sewing.

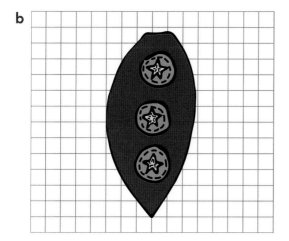

b

4. Place the felt comet trail onto a piece of turquoise felt that is slightly larger than the trail itself and pin in place. Sew around the edges of the trail, leaving the straight end open. Trim away any excess felt around the edges of the comet trail without trimming around the opening, leaving a 6mm (¼in) border around the edges so that the backing color can be seen from the front **(c)**.

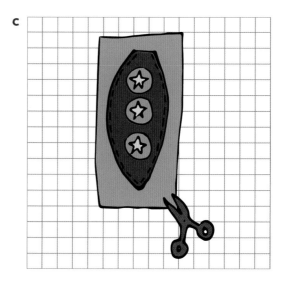

c

5. Lightly stuff the comet trail. Turn the trail on its side, pinch the opening and insert both ends of the elastic. Pin in place and sew across the opening to secure in place **(d)**.

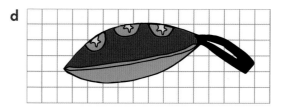

d

THE WINGED WONDER

Ever dream you could fly? With the Winged Wonder costume, you can now imagine you're flying anywhere in the world, at any time of day or night! When children dress up and pretend to play as a superhero, they are practicing helping people, community service and bravery. As the Winged Wonder you can right wrongs and save the day, or just help out in small ways that can make a big difference.

You will need

- Two 8¼ x 5⅞in (21 x 15cm) pieces of black felt for the mask

- One 5⅞ x 2½in (15 x 6.5cm) piece of red felt for the mask forehead detail

- Four 4¾ x 4⅜in (12 x 11cm) pieces of yellow felt for the mask eye detail

- One 13in (33cm) length of ⅜in (1cm) wide black elastic

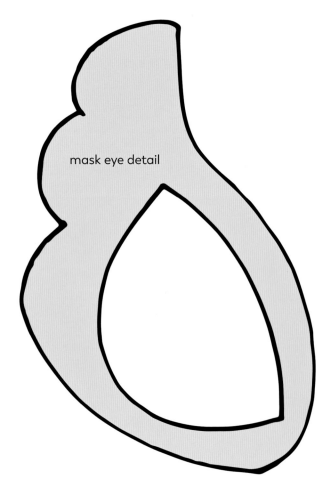

mask eye detail

1. Copy the superhero mask, mask forehead detail (see Templates), and mask eye detail templates onto paper and cut out.

2. Cut the ears from the mask template and pin the paper templates onto felt in your chosen colors **(a)**. Cut one mask piece from black felt (including the eye holes), one forehead detail piece from red felt, and two eye detail pieces from yellow felt.

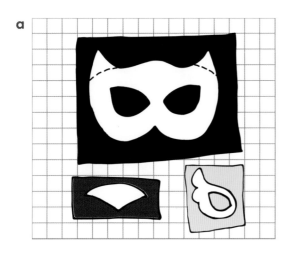

3. Glue or pin the red forehead detail to the mask and sew in place. If using glue allow it to dry completely before sewing. Glue or pin the eye detail pieces to a rectangle of yellow felt, sew in place, then trim off the excess felt backing **(b)**.

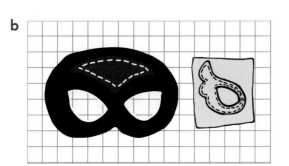

4. Place the felt superhero mask onto a piece of black felt that is slightly larger than the mask and pin the two layers together with the elastic in place on one side of the mask (marked by an 'X'), between the layers. Sew around the edges of the mask to attach the two pieces of felt together. Ensure that your elastic is not twisted as you slide the other end of it in between the layers when you get to that point on the mask, as shown by the other 'X'. Trim the excess felt all the way around your mask and carefully cut inside the eye holes **(c)**.

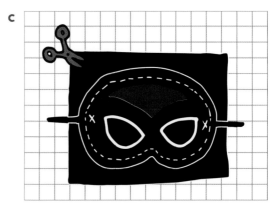

5. Position the eye details as wings on the mask, as shown. Glue or pin, and then sew them into position along the lines shown **(d)**.

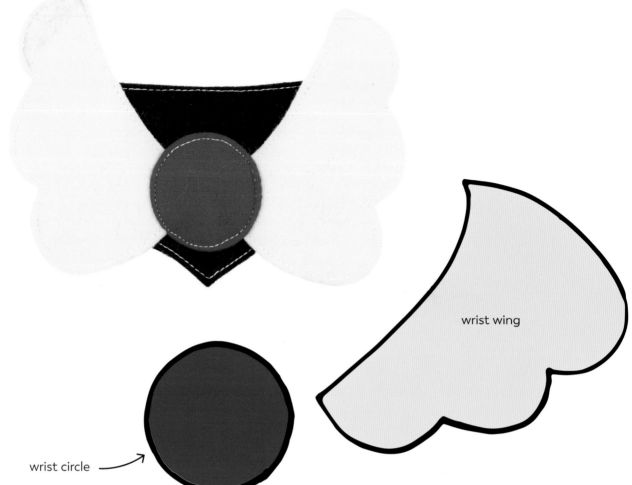

wrist circle

wrist wing

1. Copy the armband (see Templates), wrist wing and wrist circle templates onto paper and cut out.

2. Pin the paper templates onto felt in your chosen colors **(a)**. Cut two armband pieces from black felt, four wing pieces from yellow felt and two circle pieces from red felt.

You will need

- Four 8¼ x 3½in (21 x 9cm) pieces of black felt for the armbands

- Two 2 x 2in (5 x 5cm) pieces of red felt for the wrist circles

- Eight 2¾ x 4in (7 x 10cm) pieces of yellow felt for the wrist wings

- Four 1⅜in (3.5cm) strips of ¾in (2cm) wide black hook and loop fastening tape

a

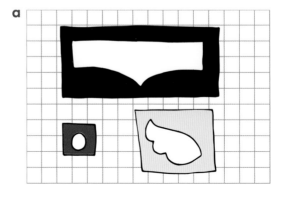

3. Place the felt armband onto a piece of black felt that is slightly larger than the armband itself and pin in place. Place one of the hook and loop fastening strips between the two layers of felt on one side, leaving some of the width sticking out from the armband. Sew around the edges, then trim away any excess felt **(b)**.

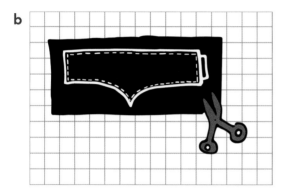

4. Glue or pin a wing piece to a rectangle of yellow felt, if gluing allow it to dry completely, then sew all round the wing **(c)**. Repeat this step to make another wing, and then trim away all the excess felt backing.

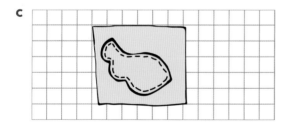

5. Place two wings, points together, in the center of the armband and place a circle over the points where they meet. Glue or pin and sew in place as shown **(d)**.

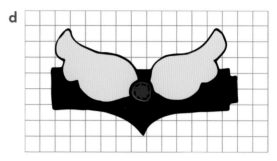

6. With the front of the armband facing downwards, place the opposite piece of hook and loop fastening on the reverse side of the armband and sew in place as shown **(e)**.

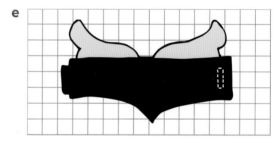

7. Repeat steps 3–6 to create a second armband.

You will need

- One 14¹⁄₂ x 6³⁄₄in (37 x 17cm) piece and one 2 x 2in (5 x 5cm) piece of red felt for the tail back and tail circle

- One 13⁷⁄₈ x 5⁷⁄₈in (35 x 15cm) piece of black felt for the tail

- Four 5¹⁄₂ x 4³⁄₈in (14 x 11cm) pieces of yellow felt for the tail wings

- One 19³⁄₄in (50cm) length of 1in (2.5cm) wide black elastic

- Polyester fiberfill stuffing

1. Copy the tail (see Templates) and tail wing and tail circle templates onto paper; cut out.

2. Pin the paper templates onto felt in your chosen colors **(a)**. Cut one tail piece from black felt, two wing pieces from yellow felt and one circle piece from red felt.

3. Glue or pin the wing pieces to rectangles of yellow felt that are slightly larger than the wing, if gluing allow it to dry completely, then sew all round the wings. Trim away all the excess felt backing **(b)**.

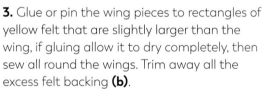

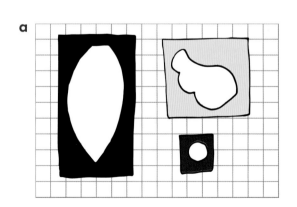

4. Pin the wing pieces in place on the black tail piece, as shown, and position the felt circle over the point where they meet before sewing around the circle to hold the wings in place. Place the winged tail onto a piece of red felt that is slightly larger than the tail itself and pin in place. Fold the wings in to prevent them getting caught in your sewing, then sew around the edges, leaving the straight end open. Trim away all the excess felt without trimming around the opening, leaving a 6mm (¼in) border around the edges **(c)**.

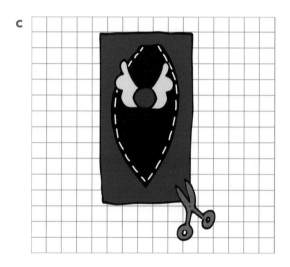

c

5. Lightly stuff the winged tail. Turn it on its side, pinch the opening and insert both ends of the elastic. Pin in place and sew across the opening to secure in place **(d)**.

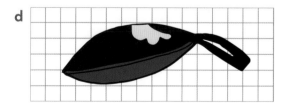

d

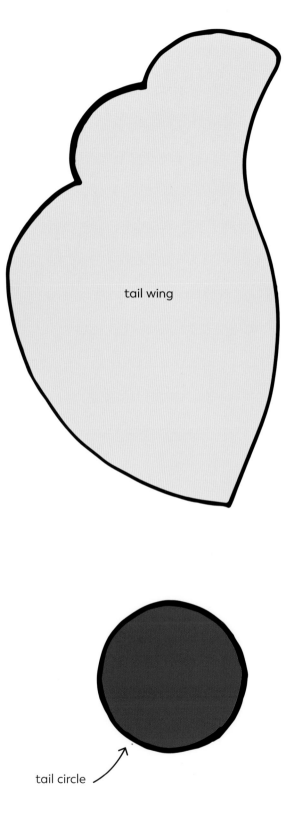

tail wing

tail circle

WILD ANIMALS

QUICK LIKE A FOX

Not only are foxes quick on their feet, but they're also quite clever! They use the Earth's magnetic field and their incredible hearing to hunt – no other animal is known to do that. While foxes act more like cats (they sleep all day, hunt at night, have retractable claws, whiskers and spines on their tongue), foxes are actually closely related to wolves. This explains why foxes and wolves are both featured in many fairy tales as quick-witted and cunning tricksters who find their way into all sorts of situations! To make this fox costume into a wolf, simply use gray felt instead of red or orange felt.

FOX MASK

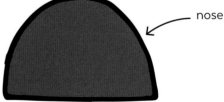

cheek

nose

You will need

- Two 8¼ x 5⅞in (21 x 15cm) pieces of auburn felt for the mask

- One 1⅝ x 1¼in (4 x 3cm) piece of brown felt for the nose

- Two 3¼ x 1⅝in (8 x 4cm) pieces of white felt for the cheeks

- One 13in (33cm) length of ⅜in (1cm) wide black elastic

1. Copy the wild animal mask (see Templates), nose and cheek templates onto paper and cut out.

2. Pin the paper templates onto felt in your chosen colors **(a)**. Cut one mask piece from auburn felt (including the eye holes), one nose piece from brown felt and two cheek pieces from white felt.

3. Glue or pin the nose and cheek pieces in position on the mask and sew in place **(b)**. If gluing pieces into place, use a very small amount of glue and wait for it to dry completely before sewing.

4. Place the felt fox mask onto a piece of auburn felt that is slightly larger than the mask and pin the two layers together with the elastic in place on one side of the mask (marked by an 'X'), between the layers. Sew around the edges of the mask to attach the two pieces of felt together. Ensure that your elastic is not twisted as you slide the other end of it in between the layers when you get to that point on the mask, as shown by the other 'X' **(c)**.

5. Trim away any excess felt around the mask and inside the eye holes **(d)**.

You will need

- Four 9½ x 10⅝in (24 x 27cm) pieces of auburn felt for the paws

- Two 9½ x 10⅝in (24 x 27cm) piece of white felt for the paw interiors

- Two 3½ x 4in (9 x 10cm) pieces and eight 2⅛ x 2½in (5.5 x 6.5cm) pieces of brown felt for the palm and toe pads

- Two 5½in (14cm) lengths of ⅜in (1cm) wide black elastic

- Polyester fiberfill stuffing

1. Copy the paw, palm pad and toe pad templates (see Templates) onto paper and cut out.

2. Pin the paper templates onto felt in your chosen colors **(a)**. Cut two paw pieces from auburn felt, two palm pad pieces from brown felt and eight toe pad pieces from brown felt.

3. Glue or pin one palm pad piece and four toe pad pieces in position onto one of the paw pieces and sew in place **(b)**. If gluing, only use a very small amount of glue and wait for it to completely dry before sewing.

a

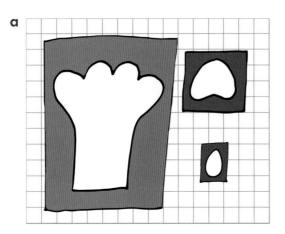

b

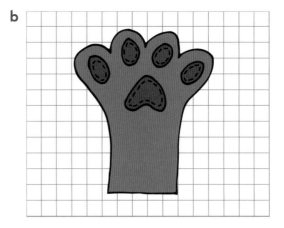

4. With the front side of the paw facing downwards, place the elastic over the wrist end of the paw and fold the felt over the top. Sew across the top of the fold to secure in place and trim any excess felt above the sewn line if necessary **(c)**.

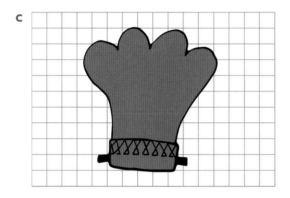

5. Place a piece of white felt that is slightly larger than the paw onto a piece of auburn felt that is the same size or larger than the white piece. Place the paw on top of the two pieces of felt and sew around the edges of the paw, leaving the wrist end and one side of the elastic open, as shown by the 'X' **(d)**.

6. Trim away any excess felt around the edges of the paw without trimming around the wrist opening **(e)**.

7. Lightly stuff the paw between the two back layers of felt and then sew these two layers of felt together.

8. Slightly pull the elastic to create a cinched effect at the wrist before sewing above the elastic. Trim away any excess felt around the wrist opening **(f)**.

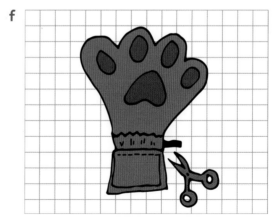

9. Repeat steps 3–8 to create a second paw.

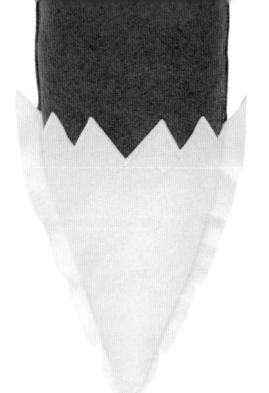

You will need

- Two 13⅞ x 5⅞in (35 x 15cm) pieces of auburn felt for the tail and tail back

- One 6¾ x 6½in (17 x 16cm) piece of white felt for the tail tip

- One 19¾in (50cm) length of 1in (2.5cm) wide black elastic

- Polyester fiberfill stuffing

1. Copy the tail (see Templates) and tail tip templates onto paper and cut out.

2. Pin the paper templates onto your selected felt colors **(a)**. Cut one tail piece from auburn felt and one tail tip piece from white felt.

3. Glue or pin the tail tip piece in position on the tail and sew in place **(b)**. If gluing, only use a very small amount of glue and wait for it to completely dry before sewing.

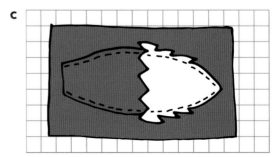

4. Place the felt fox tail onto a piece of auburn felt that is slightly larger than the tail itself and pin in place. Sew around the edges of the tail, leaving the straight end open **(c)**.

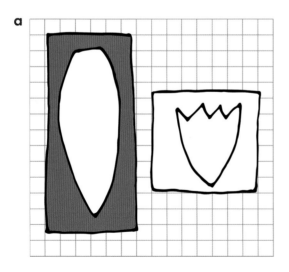

5. Trim away any excess felt around the edges of the tail without trimming around the opening, carefully cutting the tail behind the tail tip **(d)**.

6. Lightly stuff the tail. Turn the tail on its side, pinch the opening and insert both ends of the elastic. Pin in place and sew across the opening to secure in place **(e)**.

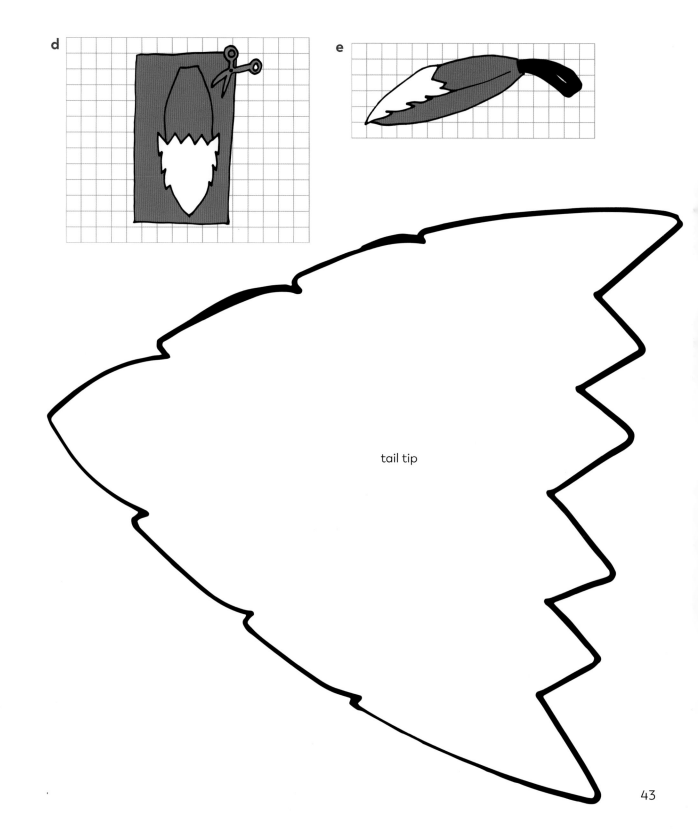

tail tip

RASCALLY LIKE A RACCOON

Raccoons are clever and very adaptable animals. These cute little creatures are often called bandits because of the black 'mask' markings on their faces as well as their knack for finding their way to food no matter the obstacles. They have been known to learn how to open doors, solve puzzles and even trick humans in order to get what they want! What kind of puzzles will you solve when you dress like a raccoon?

You will need

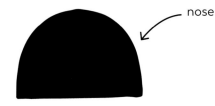

nose

eye

- Two 8⅝ x 5⅞in (22 x 15cm) pieces of light gray felt for the mask

- Two 4⅛ x 3⅜in (10.5 x 8.5cm) pieces of dark gray felt for the eyes

- One 1⅝ x 1¼in (4 x 3cm) piece of black felt for the nose

- One 13in (33cm) length of ⅜in (1cm) wide black elastic

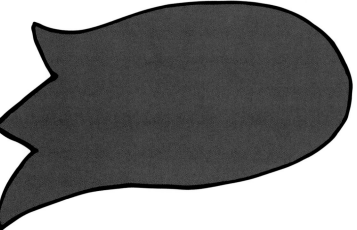

1. Copy the wild animal mask (see Templates), nose and eye templates onto paper and cut them out.

2. Pin the paper templates onto felt in your chosen colors **(a)**. Cut one mask piece from light gray felt (including the eye holes), one nose piece from black felt and two eye pieces from dark gray felt.

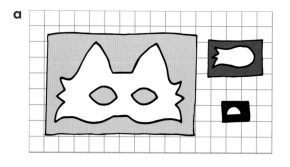

3. Glue or pin the nose and eye pieces in position on the mask and sew in place **(b)**. If gluing pieces into place, only use a small amount of glue and wait for it to dry completely before sewing.

4. Place the felt raccoon mask onto a piece of light gray felt that is slightly larger than the mask and pin the two layers together with the elastic in place on one side of the mask (marked by an 'X'), between the layers. Sew around the edges of the mask to attach the two pieces of felt together. Ensure that your elastic is not twisted as you slide the other end of it in between the layers when you get to that point on the mask, as shown by the other 'X' **(c)**.

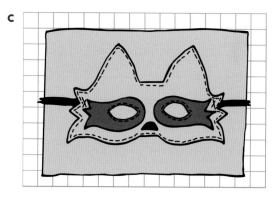

5. Trim away any excess felt around the mask and inside the eye holes **(d)**.

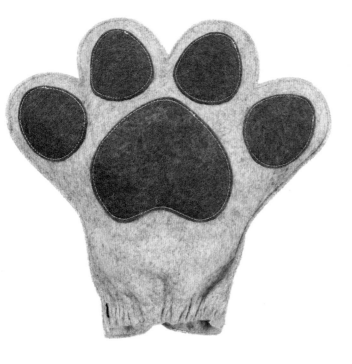

You will need

- Six 9$\frac{1}{2}$ x 10$\frac{5}{8}$in (24 x 27cm) pieces of light gray felt for the paws and paw interiors

- Two 3$\frac{1}{2}$ x 4in (9 x 10cm) pieces and eight 2$\frac{1}{8}$ x 2$\frac{1}{2}$in (5.5 x 6.5cm) pieces of dark gray felt for the palm and toe pads

- Two 5$\frac{1}{2}$in (14cm) lengths of $\frac{3}{8}$in (1cm) wide black elastic

- Polyester fiberfill stuffing

1. Copy the paw, palm pad and toe pad templates (see Templates) onto paper and cut them out.

2. Pin the paper templates onto felt in your chosen colors **(a)**. Cut two paw pieces from light gray felt, two palm pad pieces from dark gray felt and eight toe pad pieces from dark gray felt.

3. Glue or pin one palm pad piece and four toe pad pieces in position onto one of the paw pieces and sew in place **(b)**. If gluing, only use a very small amount of glue and wait for it to dry completely before sewing.

b

a

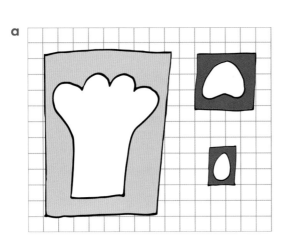

4. With the front side of the paw facing downwards, place the elastic over the wrist end of the paw and fold the felt over the top. Sew across the top of the fold to secure in place and trim any excess felt above the sewn line if necessary **(c)**.

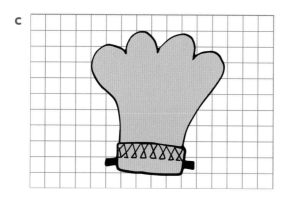

c

5. Place a piece of light gray felt that is slightly larger than the paw onto a piece of light gray felt that is the same size or larger than it. Place the paw on top of the two pieces of felt and sew around the edges of the paw, leaving the wrist end and one side of the elastic open, as shown by the 'X' **(d)**.

d

6. Trim away any excess felt around the edges of the paw without trimming around the wrist opening **(e)**.

e

7. Lightly stuff the paw between the two back layers of felt and then sew these two layers of felt together.

8. Slightly pull the elastic to create a cinched effect at the wrist before sewing above the elastic. Trim away any excess felt around the wrist opening **(f)**.

f

9. Repeat steps 3–8 to create a second paw.

You will need

- Two 13⅞ x 5⅞in (35 x 15cm) pieces of light gray felt for the tail and tail back

- Three 5⅛ x 3⅜in (13 x 8.5cm) pieces of dark gray felt for the stripes

- One 19¾in (50cm) length of 1in (2.5cm) wide black elastic

- Polyester fiberfill stuffing

top/bottom tail stripes

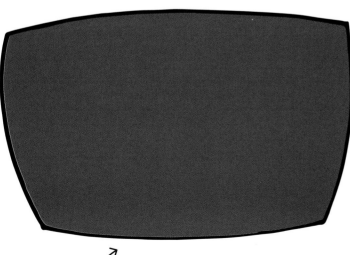

middle tail stripe

1. Copy the tail (see Templates) and both raccoon tail stripe templates onto paper and cut them out.

2. Pin the paper templates onto felt in your chosen colors **(a)**. Cut one tail piece from light gray felt, and one middle tail stripe piece and two top/bottom tail stripe pieces from dark gray felt.

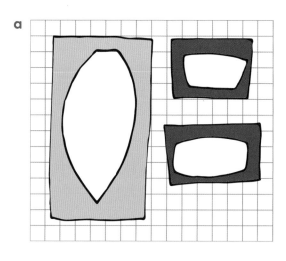

3. Glue or pin the tail stripe pieces in position on the tail and sew in place **(b)**. If gluing, only use a very small amount of glue and wait for it to dry completely before sewing.

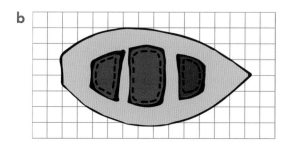

4. Place the felt raccoon tail onto a piece of light gray felt that is slightly larger than the tail itself and pin in place. Sew around the edges of the tail, leaving the straight end open. Trim away any excess felt around the edges of the tail without trimming around the opening **(c)**.

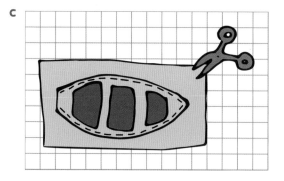

5. Lightly stuff the tail. Turn the tail on its side, pinch the opening and insert both ends of the elastic. Pin in place and sew across the opening to secure in place **(d)**.

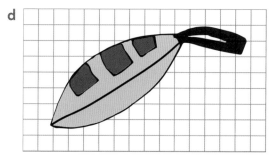

DYNAMIC LIKE A TIGER

Tigers are both strong in body and solid in character. They are solitary animals and the largest cats in the world. Tigers are excellent swimmers and fast runners, which make them very intimidating hunters. Tigers are the only cat species that are completely striped; they even have stripes on their skin! The unique stripes help camouflage the tiger while stalking prey in the tall grasses. Try sneaking up on someone and give them a growl!

You will need

- Two 8⅝ x 5⅞in (22 x 15cm) pieces of orange felt for the mask
- Two 4⅜ x 2¾in (11 x 7cm) pieces of white felt for the cheeks
- Two 2½ x 2⅛in (6.5 x 5.5cm) pieces, two 1⅜ x 1¼in (3.5 x 3cm) pieces, four 1⅝ x 1¼in (4 x 3cm) pieces and one 1¾ x 1⅜in (4.5 x 3.5cm) piece of black felt for the stripes and nose
- One 13in (33cm) length of ⅜in (1cm) wide black elastic

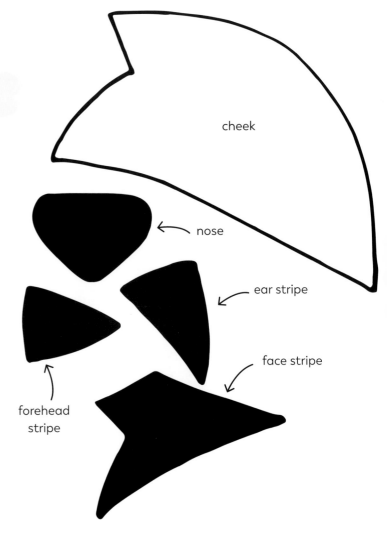

cheek

nose

ear stripe

face stripe

forehead stripe

1. Copy the wild animal mask (see Templates), the nose, cheek and ear, face and forehead stripe templates onto paper and cut them out.

2. Pin the paper templates onto felt in your chosen colors **(a)**. Cut one mask piece from orange felt (including the eye holes), one nose piece from black felt, two cheek pieces from white felt and the following stripe pieces from black felt: four ear stripes, two forehead stripes and two face stripes.

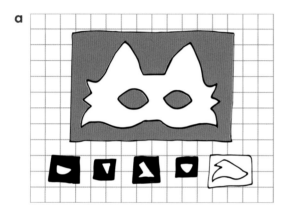

3. Glue or pin the black stripe pieces in position on the mask and sew in place **(b)**. If gluing pieces into place, only use a small amount of glue and wait for it to dry completely before sewing.

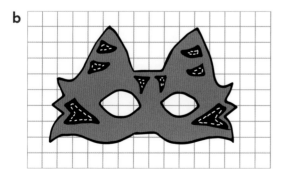

4. Place the felt tiger mask onto a piece of orange felt that is slightly larger than the mask, with the white cheek pieces between the mask and the backing, positioned so they can be seen below the bottom edge. Pin or glue in place.

5. Pin together the two layers of the mask with the elastic in place on one side of the mask (marked by an 'X'), between the layers. Sew around the edges of the mask to attach the two pieces of felt together. Ensure that your elastic is not twisted as you slide the other end of it in between the layers when you get to that point on the mask, as shown by the other 'X'. Then pin or glue the nose, and sew it in place **(c)**.

6. Trim away any excess felt around the edges of the mask and inside the eyes **(d)**.

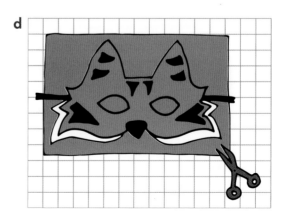

You will need

- Six 9½ x 10⅝in (24 x 27cm) pieces of orange felt for the paws and paw interiors

- Two 3½ x 4in (9 x 10cm) pieces and eight 2⅛ x 2½in (5.5 x 6.5cm) pieces of black felt for the palm and toe pads

- Two 5½in (14cm) lengths of ⅜in (1cm) wide black elastic

- Polyester fiberfill stuffing

1. Copy the paw, palm pad and toe pad templates (see Templates) onto paper and cut them out.

2. Pin the paper templates onto felt in your chosen colors **(a)**. Cut two paw pieces from orange felt, two palm pad pieces from black felt and eight toe pad pieces from black felt.

3. Glue or pin one palm pad piece and four toe pad pieces in position onto one of the paw pieces and sew in place **(b)**. If gluing, only use a very small amount of glue and wait for it to dry completely before sewing.

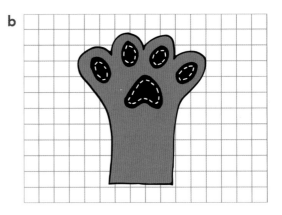

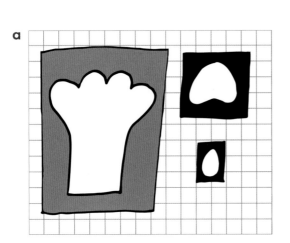

4. With the front side of the paw facing downwards, place the elastic over the wrist end of the paw and fold the felt over the top. Sew across the top of the fold to secure in place and trim any excess felt above the sewn line if necessary **(c)**.

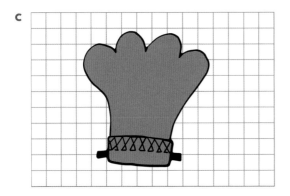

5. Place a piece of orange felt that is slightly larger than the paw onto a piece of orange felt that is the same size or larger than it. Place the paw on top of the two pieces of felt and sew around the edges of the paw, leaving the wrist end and one side of the elastic open, as shown by the 'X' **(d)**.

6. Trim away any excess felt around the edges of the paw without trimming around the wrist opening **(e)**.

7. Lightly stuff the paw between the two back layers of felt and then sew these two layers of felt together.

8. Slightly pull the elastic to create a cinched effect at the wrist before sewing above the elastic. Trim away any excess felt around the wrist opening **(f)**.

9. Repeat steps 3–8 to create a second paw.

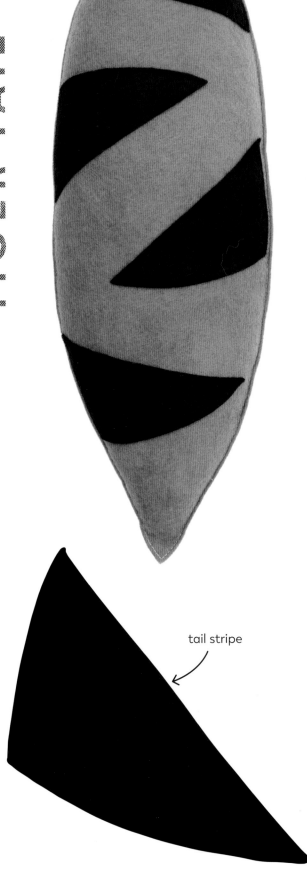

You will need

- Two 13⁷⁄₈ x 5⁷⁄₈in (35 x 15cm) pieces of orange felt for the tail and tail back

- Four 4³⁄₄ x 3¹⁄₄in (12 x 8cm) pieces of black felt for the stripes

- One 19³⁄₄in (50cm) length of 1in (2.5cm) wide black elastic

- Polyester fiberfill stuffing

1. Copy the tail template (see Templates) and tail stripe template onto paper and then cut them out.

2. Pin the paper templates onto felt in your chosen colors **(a)**. Cut one tail piece from orange felt and four tail stripe pieces from black felt.

tail stripe

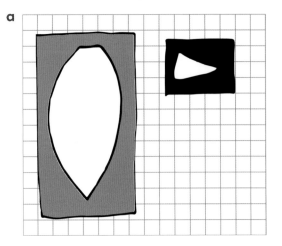

3. Glue or pin the tail stripe pieces in position on the tail and sew in place **(b)**. If gluing, only use a very small amount of glue and wait for it to dry completely before sewing.

5. Lightly stuff the tail. Turn the tail on its side, pinch the opening and insert both ends of the elastic. Pin in place and sew across the opening to secure in place **(d)**.

b

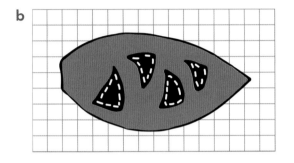

d

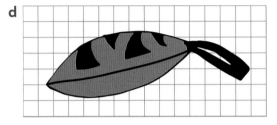

4. Place the felt tiger tail onto a piece of orange felt that is slightly larger than the tail itself and pin in place. Sew around the edges of the tail, leaving the straight end open. Trim away any excess felt around the edges of the tail without trimming around the opening **(c)**.

c

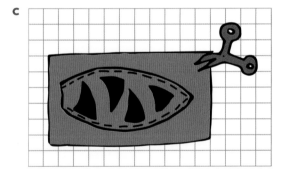

By changing the orange felt for white you could create your own version of the rare white tiger. White tigers are not a separate species but a genetic anomly, mysterious and beautiful.

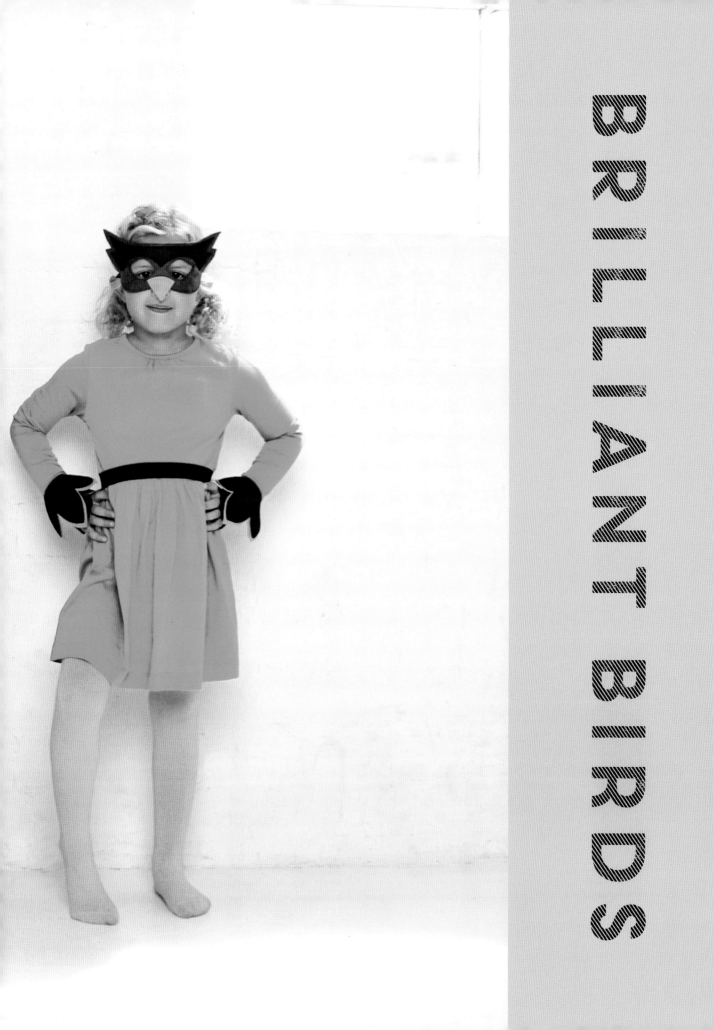

BRILLIANT BIRDS

PRECOCIOUS LIKE A PARROT

Parrots come in many shapes and sizes and are often very brightly colored. They are curious and intelligent birds, qualities that give them the ability to adapt to new situations and environments. Curiosity fuels inquisitive thinking and inspires exploration and learning. This ability to adapt and learn gives parrots the opportunity to interact with humans on a deeper level than most animals. Curiosity makes you smarter! The more you WANT to learn, the more you WILL learn!

large head feathers

You will need

- Two 9½ x 4⅜in (24 x 11cm) pieces of red felt for the mask

- Two 5⅞ x 3⅜in (15 x 8.5cm) pieces of turquoise felt for the large head feathers

- One 4⅜ x 2in (11 x 5cm) piece of green felt for the small head feathers

- Two 2 x 2in (5 x 5cm) pieces of white felt for the face feathers

- Three 2½ x 2¾in (6.5 x 7cm) pieces of yellow felt for the beak

- One 13in (33cm) length of ⅜in (1cm) wide black elastic

upper beak

face feathers

lower beak

small head feathers

1. Copy the bird mask (see Templates), upper and lower beak and all the feathers templates onto paper and cut them out.

2. Pin the paper templates onto your selected felt colors **(a)**. Cut the mask from red felt, including cutting out the eye holes, then cut one large head feathers piece from turquoise felt, one small head feathers piece from green felt, two face feathers pieces from white felt, one upper beak and one lower beak from yellow felt.

4. Place the felt parrot mask onto a rectangle of red felt, which is slightly larger than the mask itself and pin the two layers together with the elastic in place on one side of the mask (marked by an 'X'), between the layers. Sew around the edges of the mask to attach the two pieces of felt together. Ensure that your elastic is not twisted as you slide the other end of it in between the layers when you get to that point on the mask, as shown by the other 'X'. Trim the excess felt all the way around your mask and carefully cut inside the eye holes **(c)**.

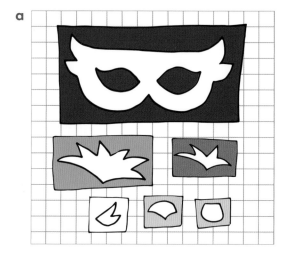

a

c

3. Pin or glue the white face feathers pieces into position on the mask and sew them in place **(b)**. Sew the two beak pieces together onto a small square of yellow felt, and sew the head feathers pieces together in the same way onto a small piece of backing felt. If gluing pieces into place, use a very small amount and wait for the glue to dry before sewing. Trim the excess backing felt from the head feathers and beak, and set aside.

5. Sew the head feathers and beak to the parrot mask, positioning them as shown **(d)**.

d

b

- Two 8¼ x 3½in (21 x 9cm) pieces of red felt for the armband

- Two 8¼ x 4¾in (21 x 12cm) pieces of turquoise felt for the feather backing

- Two 4¾ x 4½in (12 x 11.5cm) pieces of green felt for the feather detail

- Two 4¾ x 4½in (12 x 11.5cm) pieces of white felt for the feather detail backing

- Four 1⅜in (3.5cm) strips of ¾in (2cm) wide black hook and loop fastening tape

1. Copy the template for the armband, the parrot wing feather backing (see Templates) and the wing feather detail onto paper, then cut them out.

2. Pin all the paper templates to your selected felt colors **(a)**. Cut two armband pieces from red felt, two feather backing pieces from turquoise felt and two feather detail pieces from green felt.

3. Pin or glue one felt armband onto a feather backing piece; the backing will be slightly larger than the armband itself. Sew the felt armband onto the feather backing, inserting a piece of hook and loop fastening tape at one end as shown and sewing that in as you stitch the feather backing to the armband. Trim the excess felt from around the top and sides of the armband leaving the feathered backing at the bottom **(b)**.

a
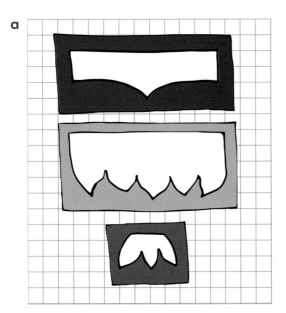

b
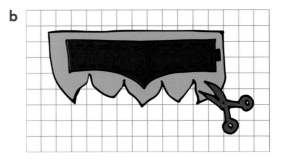

4. Pin or glue the green feather detail onto a white rectangle of felt and sew it in place **(c)**, then trim the backing felt so that about 3mm (⅛in) shows all the way around the feather detail, except on the top straight edge, which should be trimmed level with the top of the feather detail.

5. Sew the feather detail to the top of the armband **(d)**.

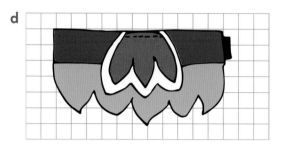

6. Turn the armband over and sew the opposite piece of hook and loop fastening in position on the reverse side as shown **(e)**.

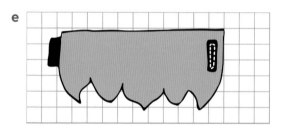

7. Repeat steps 3–6 to create a second wing.

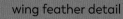

wing feather detail

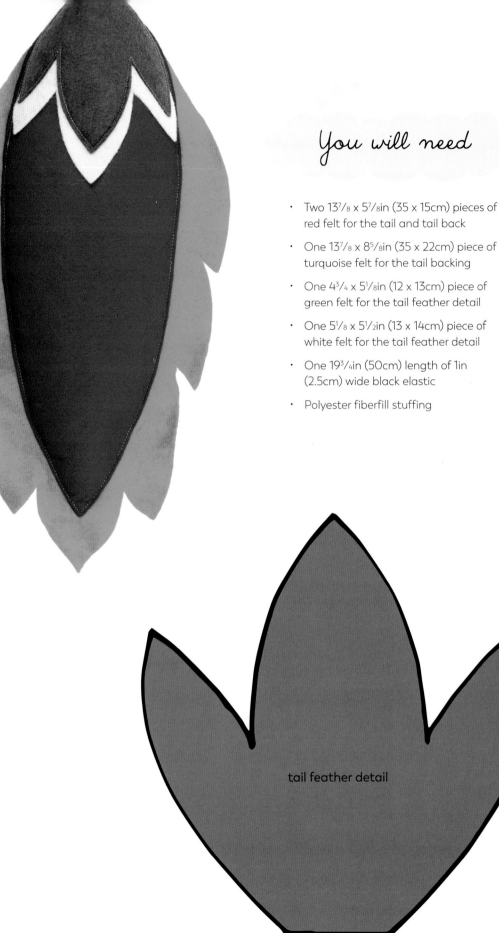

You will need

- Two 13⅞ x 5⅞in (35 x 15cm) pieces of red felt for the tail and tail back

- One 13⅞ x 8⅝in (35 x 22cm) piece of turquoise felt for the tail backing

- One 4¾ x 5⅛in (12 x 13cm) piece of green felt for the tail feather detail

- One 5⅛ x 5½in (13 x 14cm) piece of white felt for the tail feather detail

- One 19¾in (50cm) length of 1in (2.5cm) wide black elastic

- Polyester fiberfill stuffing

tail feather detail

1. Copy the template for the tail, the parrot tail backing (see Templates), and tail feather detail onto paper and cut them out.

2. Pin all the paper templates to your selected felt colors and carefully cut them out **(a)**. Cut one tail piece from red felt, one tail backing piece from turquoise felt, one tail feather detail piece from white felt and one tail feather detail piece from green felt.

3. Pin or glue the tail feather detail pieces to the tail as shown, with the green feather on top and the white one beneath. Sew around just the green top layer of feathers **(b)**.

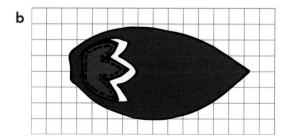

4. Place the parrot tail onto the tail backing (the backing is slightly larger than the tail itself), then position everything on top of a rectangle of red felt. Sew all the pieces together following the outline of the basic red tail piece, and leaving an opening at the straight end for stuffing **(c)**.

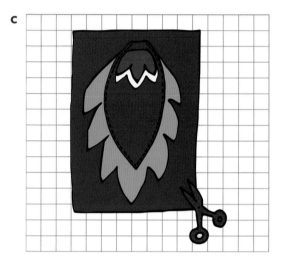

5. Trim the excess from the bottom rectangle to match the shape of the basic tail. Do not trim the turquoise tail backing feathers!

6. Lightly stuff the tail then turn it on its side, pinch the opening and insert both ends of the elastic. Pin in place and sew across the opening to secure the elastic in position **(d)**.

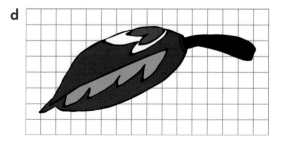

WISE LIKE AN OWL

Owls have big eyes and mysterious dispositions that have caused them to symbolize everything from wisdom to terror throughout history. On silent wings, an owl can swoop through the night, making it a brilliant creature to 'be' if you're exploring dreams, or the night-time forest. What will you see with your huge owl eyes?

You will need

- Two 9¹⁄₂ x 4³⁄₈in (24 x 11cm) pieces of light brown felt for the mask

- One 9 x 2³⁄₄in (23 x 7cm) piece of dark brown felt for the head feathers

- Two 2¹⁄₈ x 2in (5.5 x 5cm) pieces of yellow felt for the beak

- One 13in (33cm) length of ³⁄₈in (1cm) wide black elastic

beak

Old Brown, the owl in Beatrix Potter's The Tale of Squirrel Nutkin, was a wise old bird, but also a bit cranky. Cheeky Squirrel Nutkin asked him several riddles... Can your wise owl answer riddles? Or make them up?

1. Copy the template for the bird mask, the owl head feathers (see Templates) and beak onto paper. Cut them out carefully.

2. Pin the paper templates to your selected felt colors **(a)**. Cut one mask piece from light brown felt (including the eye holes), one head feathers piece from dark brown felt and one beak from yellow felt.

3. Pin or glue the head feathers piece to the owl mask. If you are gluing pieces into place, use only a very small amount and wait for the glue to dry completely before sewing the pieces. Then sew the head feathers piece into place. Sew the beak to a rectangle of yellow felt, then trim around it and set aside **(b)**.

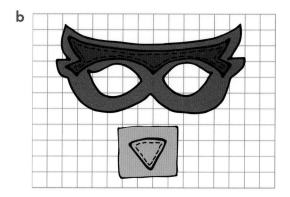

4. Place the felt owl mask onto a rectangle of light brown felt, slightly larger than the mask itself, and pin the two layers together with the elastic in place on one side of the mask (marked by an 'X'), between the layers. Sew around the edges of the mask to attach the two pieces of felt together. Ensure that your elastic is not twisted as you slide the other end of it in between the layers when you get to that point on the mask, as shown by the other 'X'. Trim the excess felt all the way around your mask and carefully cut inside the eye holes **(c)**.

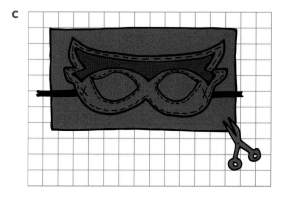

5. Sew the beak into position onto the owl mask as shown **(d)**.

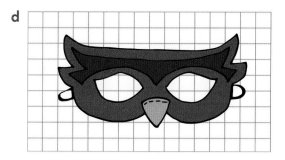

You will need

- Two 8¹/₄ x 3¹/₂in (21 x 9cm) pieces of light brown felt for the armbands
- Two 8¹/₄ x 4³/₄in (21 x 12cm) pieces and two 4³/₄ x 4¹/₂in (12 x 11.5cm) pieces of dark brown felt for the wing feather backing and wing feather details
- Two 4³/₄ x 4¹/₂in (12 x 11.5cm) pieces of yellow felt for the wing feather detail backing
- Four 1³/₈in (3.5cm) strips of ³/₄in (2cm) wide black hook and loop fastening tape

1. Copy the template for the armband, the owl wing feather backing (see Templates) and wing feather detail onto paper, then cut them out.

2. Pin all the paper templates to your selected felt colors **(a)**. Cut two armband pieces from light brown felt, two feather backing pieces from dark brown felt, and two feather detail pieces from dark brown felt.

3. Place one felt armband onto a feather backing piece, which will be slightly larger than the armband itself. Sew the felt armband onto the feather backing, inserting a piece of hook and loop fastening at one end as shown and sewing that in as you stitch the feather backing to the armband. Trim the excess felt from around the top and sides of the armband **(b)**.

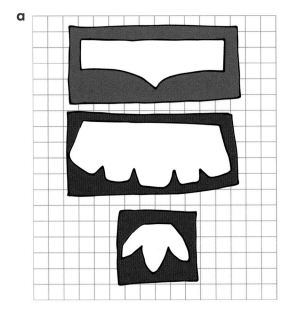

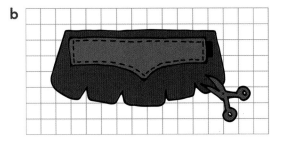

74

4. Pin or glue the feather detail onto a rectangle of yellow felt and sew it in place **(c)**, then trim the backing felt so that about 3mm (⅛in) shows all the way around the feather detail, except on the top straight edge, which should be trimmed level with the top of the feather detail.

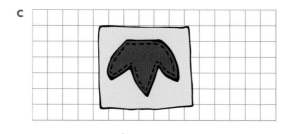

5. Sew the feather detail to the top of the armband **(d)**.

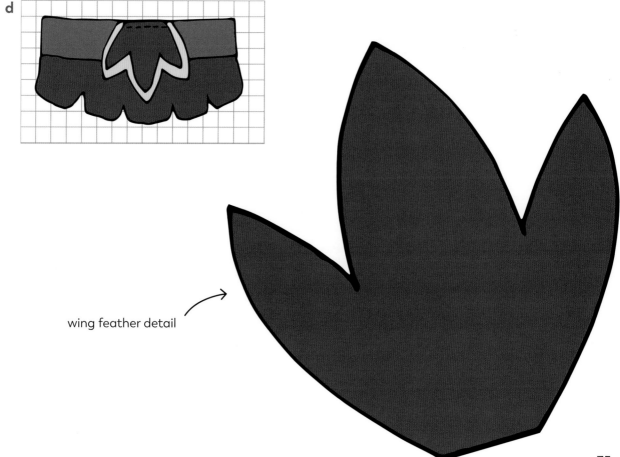

6. Turn the armband over and sew the opposite piece of hook and loop fastening in position on the reverse side as shown **(e)**.

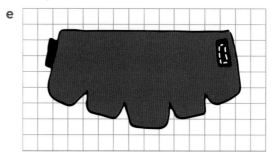

7. Repeat steps 3–6 to create a second wing.

wing feather detail

1. Copy the template for the tail, the owl tail backing and owl tail detail (see Templates) onto paper and then cut them out.

2. Pin all the paper templates to your selected felt colors and carefully cut them out **(a)**. Cut one tail from light brown felt, one tail backing from dark brown felt and one tail detail from dark brown felt.

You will need

- Two 13⁷⁄₈ x 5⁷⁄₈in (35 x 15cm) pieces of light brown felt for the tail and tail back

- One 13 x 10⁵⁄₈in (33 x 27cm) piece and one 10⁵⁄₈ x 5¹⁄₈in (27 x 13cm) piece of dark brown felt for the tail backing and tail detail

- One 19³⁄₄in (50cm) length of 1in (2.5cm) wide black elastic

- Polyester fiberfill stuffing

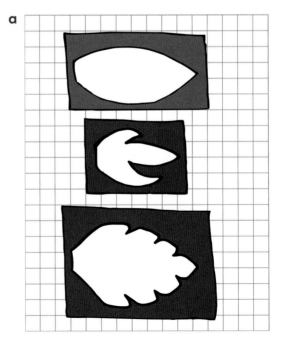

a

3. Glue or pin the feather detail piece to the tail. If gluing, wait until it is completely dry. Sew it in place **(b)**.

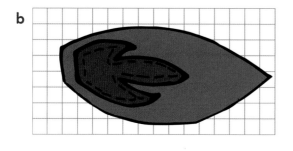

b

4. Place the owl tail onto the tail backing (the backing is slightly larger than the tail itself), then position everything on top of a larger rectangle of light brown felt. Sew all the pieces together following the outline of the basic light brown tail piece, and leaving an opening at the straight end for stuffing. Trim the excess from the bottom rectangle to match the shape of the basic tail **(c)**. Do not trim the tail backing feathers!

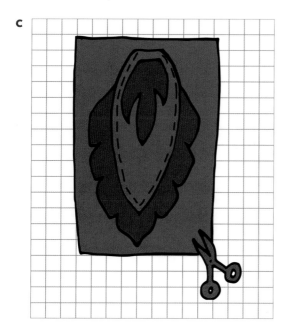

c

5. Lightly stuff the tail, then turn it on its side, pinch the opening and insert both ends of the elastic. Pin in place and sew across the opening to secure the elastic in position **(d)**.

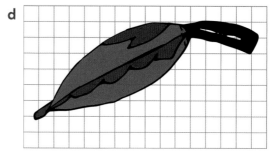

d

Owls have fixed eye sockets, so they can't swivel their eyes. It helps to keep their vision steady when they hunt in flight, but it means they have to stretch their necks right round to look behind them.

STRUT LIKE A PEACOCK

Peacocks wear a crown of feathers on their heads and a train of feathers many feet long that drag behind as they strut to impress! The strut paired with the impressively large extended tail feathers has made the peacock a symbol of pride and confidence. And who wouldn't feel like the star of the show with all those dazzling colors on display? Can you strut proudly like a peacock while wearing your new peacock costume?

You will need

- Two 9½ x 4⅜in (24 x 11cm) pieces of mint felt for the mask

- Two 7½ x 3¼in (19 x 8cm) pieces of turquoise felt for the feather crown

- Two 1⅝ x 2in (4 x 5cm) pieces of pale pink felt for the eye details

- One 1¾ x 3in (4.5 x 7.5cm) piece of purple felt for the feather crown center

- Two 2 x 2¾in (5 x 7cm) pieces of black felt for the beak

- One 13in (33cm) length of ⅜in (1cm) wide black elastic

1. Copy the template for the bird mask (see Templates), the eye detail, feather crown and feather crown center, and the beak onto paper. Cut them out carefully.

2. Pin the paper templates to your selected felt colors **(a)**. Cut one bird mask piece from mint felt (remembering to cut out the eye holes), one feather crown piece from turquoise felt, one feather crown center piece from purple felt, one beak piece from black felt and two eye details from pale pink felt.

beak ←

a

3. Pin or glue the eye details to the peacock mask. If you are gluing pieces into place, use only a small amount and wait for the glue to completely dry before sewing the pieces. Then sew the eye details into place **(b)**. Sew the beak to a rectangle of black felt. Layer and sew the feather crown and feather crown center onto another rectangle of turquoise felt. Trim around both these pieces; set aside.

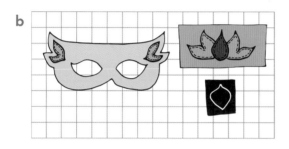

b

4. Place the felt peacock mask onto a mint felt rectangle, slightly larger than the mask itself, and pin the two layers together with the elastic in place on one side of the mask (marked by an 'X'), between the layers. Sew around the edges of the mask to attach the two pieces of felt together. Ensure that your elastic is not twisted as you slide the other end of it in between the layers when you get to that point on the mask, as shown by the other 'X'. Trim the excess felt all the way around your mask and carefully cut inside the eye holes **(c)**.

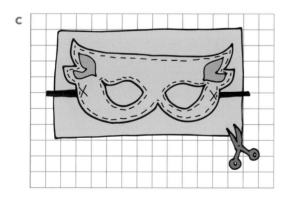

c

5. Sew the beak and the feather crown onto the peacock mask as shown **(d)**.

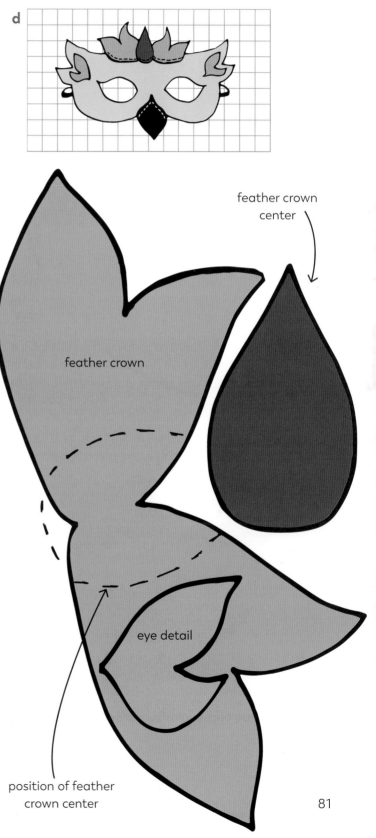

d

feather crown center

feather crown

eye detail

position of feather crown center

You will need

- Two 8¼ x 3½in (21 x 9cm) pieces of mint felt for the armbands

- Two 8¼ x 4¾in (21 x 12cm) pieces of turquoise felt for the wing feather backing

- Two 3¾ x 4in (9.5 x 10cm) pieces of purple felt for the feather detail

- Two 4 x 4⅛in (10 x 10.5cm) pieces of pale pink felt for the feather detail backing

- Four 1⅜in (3.5cm) strips of ¾in (2cm) wide black hook and loop fastening tape

1. Copy the template for the armband, peacock wing feather backing (see Templates) and feather detail onto paper, then cut out.

2. Pin all the paper templates to your selected felt colors **(a)**. Cut two armband pieces from mint felt, two peacock feather backing pieces from turquoise felt, and two feather detail pieces from purple felt.

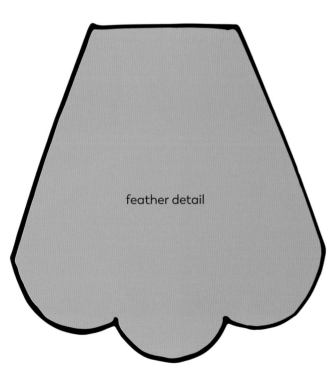

feather detail

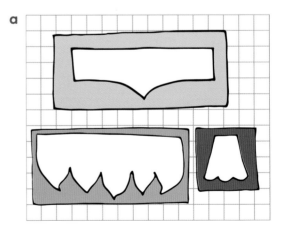

a

3. Place one felt armband onto a feather backing piece, which will be slightly larger than the armband itself. Sew the felt armband onto the feather backing, inserting a piece of hook and loop fastening at one end as shown and sewing that in as you stitch the feather backing to the armband. Trim the excess felt from around the top and sides of the armband **(b)**.

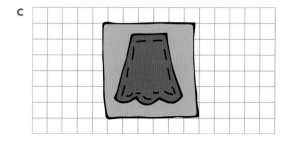

4. Pin or glue the feather detail onto a pale pink rectangle of felt and sew it in place **(c)**, then trim the backing felt so that about 3mm (1/8in) shows all the way around the feather detail, except on the top straight edge, which should be trimmed level with the top of the feather detail.

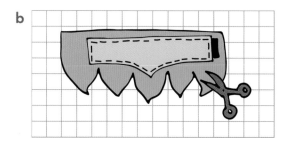

5. Sew the feather detail to the top of the armband **(d)**.

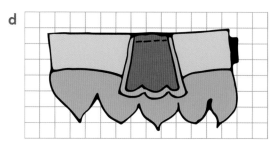

6. Turn the armband over and sew the opposite piece of hook and loop fastening in position on the reverse side as shown **(e)**.

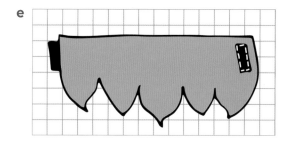

7. Repeat steps 3–6 to create a second wing.

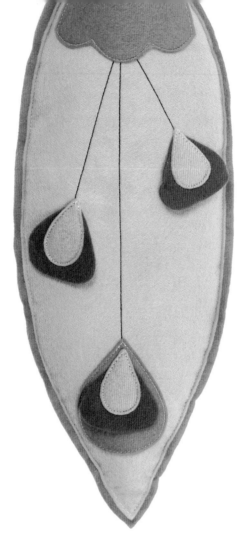

You will need

- One 13⅞ x 5⅞in (35 x 15cm) piece of mint felt for the tail

- One 14½ x 6¾in (37 x 17cm) piece, one 3¾ x 3½in (9.5 x 9cm) piece and one 2½ x 3in (6.5 x 7.5cm) piece of turquoise felt for the tail back, feather detail and large tail feather

- Three 2⅛ x 2⅛in (5.5 x 5.5cm) pieces of purple felt for the medium tail feathers

- Three 1⅜ x 1¾in (3.5 x 4.5cm) pieces of pink felt for the small tail feathers

- Black sewing thread

- One 19¾in (50cm) length of 1in (2.5cm) wide black elastic

- Polyester fiberfill stuffing

1. Copy the tail template (see Templates), the feather detail and the three different tail feathers onto paper and cut them out.

2. Pin all the paper templates to the colored felt and cut them out **(a)**. Cut one tail piece in mint, one feather detail piece in turquoise, one large tail feather piece in turquoise, three medium tail feather pieces in purple and three small tail feather pieces in pale pink.

3. Sew three lines in black thread from the straight edge of the tail towards the tip as shown **(b)**.

b

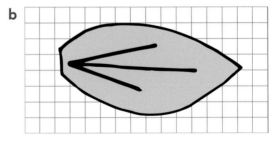

a

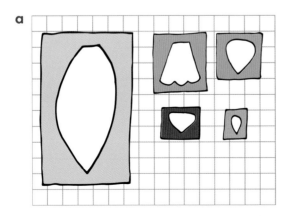

4. Pin or glue the feather detail and tail feathers in place, layering the tail feathers as shown **(c)**. If gluing, ensure it is completely dry before sewing all the pieces in place.

6. Lightly stuff the tail, then turn it on its side, pinch the opening and insert both ends of the elastic. Pin in place and sew across the opening to secure the elastic in position **(e)**.

c

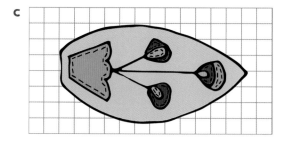

e

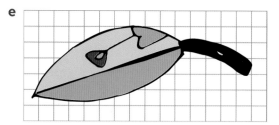

5. Place the peacock tail onto a rectangle of turquoise felt that is slightly larger than the tail itself. Sew round the edge of the tail, leaving an opening at the straight end for stuffing **(d)**. Trim the bottom rectangle to 6mm (¼in) larger than the tail so that the backing color shows all round the edges.

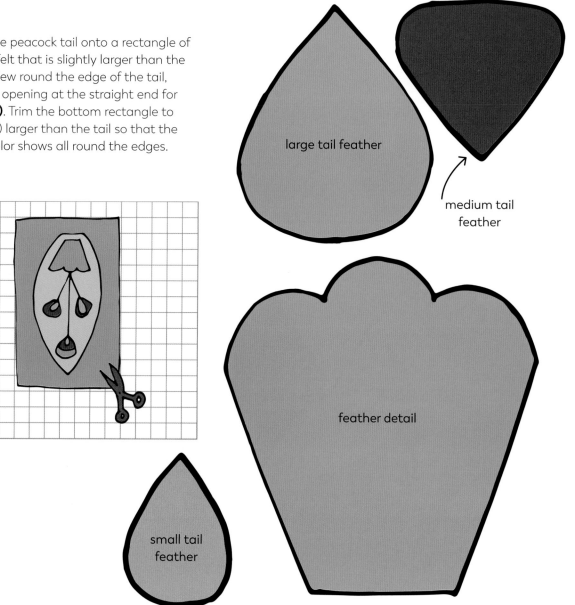

large tail feather

medium tail feather

feather detail

d

small tail feather

85

ENCHANTING AS A UNICORN

Unicorns are enchanted creatures that grant wishes for believers and are the perfect way to sprinkle a little magic into your life! Dressing up in costume is a way for us to escape our daily stresses, especially if you're dressing as a magical unicorn! Unicorns are believed to bring good fortune to those who touch their horn. When you dress up as a unicorn, what good fortune will you bestow on those around you?

You will need

- Two 8¼ x 8⅝in (21 x 22cm) pieces of pink felt for the mask

- One 8¼ x 3½in (21 x 9cm) piece and one 4⅜ x 2¾in (11 x 7cm) piece of purple felt for the bangs (fringe) and muzzle

- Two 2½ x 4½in (6.5 x 11.5cm) pieces of yellow felt for the horn

- Two 1 x 1in (2.5 x 2.5cm) pieces of mint felt for the heart nostrils

- One 13in (33cm) length of ⅜in (1cm) wide black elastic

1. Copy the mythical creature mask, unicorn bangs (fringe), unicorn horn (see Templates), muzzle and heart nostril templates onto paper and cut them out.

2. Pin the paper templates onto felt in your chosen colors **(a)**. Cut one mask piece from pink felt (including the eye holes), one muzzle piece and bangs (fringe) piece from pale purple felt, one horn from yellow felt and two heart nostrils from mint felt.

a

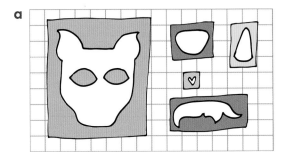

3. Glue or pin the hearts onto the muzzle, glue or pin the muzzle to the mask and sew in place **(b)**. If gluing pieces into place, only use a small amount of glue and wait for it to dry completely before sewing. Place the horn onto a rectangle of yellow felt and sew around the edge; trim away the excess felt and set aside.

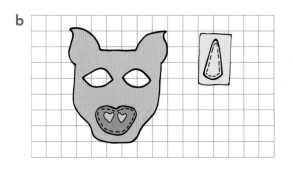

b

4. Place the felt unicorn mask onto a piece of pink felt that is slightly larger than the mask and pin the two layers together with the elastic in place on one side of the mask (marked by an 'X'), between the layers. Sew around the edges of the mask to attach the two pieces of felt together. Ensure that your elastic is not twisted as you slide the other end of it in between the layers when you get to that point on the mask, as shown by the other 'X' **(c)**.

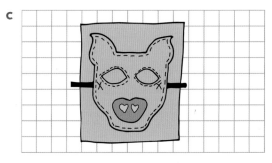

c

5. Glue or pin the bangs (fringe) piece to the mask as shown and sew around it. Trim away any excess felt around the edges of the mask and inside the eye holes **(d)**.

d

6. Position the horn on the mask and sew at the base as shown **(e)**.

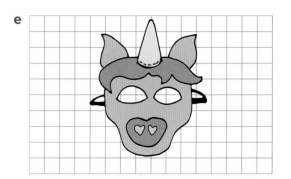

e

muzzle

heart nostril

You will need

- Six 9$\frac{1}{2}$ x 10$\frac{5}{8}$in (24 x 27cm) pieces of pink felt for the paws and paw interiors

- Two 3$\frac{1}{2}$ x 3$\frac{1}{2}$in (9 x 9cm) pieces and eight 2$\frac{1}{8}$ x 2$\frac{1}{2}$in (5.5 x 6.5cm) pieces of pale purple felt for the palm and toe pads

- Eight 2$\frac{1}{8}$ x 2$\frac{1}{2}$in (5.5 x 6.5cm) pieces of mint felt for the nails

- Two 5$\frac{1}{2}$in (14cm) lengths of $\frac{3}{8}$in (1cm) wide black elastic

- Polyester fiberfill stuffing

1. Copy the paw, the toe pad and the unicorn palm pad templates (see Templates) and the nails template onto paper and cut them out.

2. Pin the paper templates onto felt in your chosen colors **(a)**. Cut two paw pieces from pink felt, two palm pad pieces and eight toe pad pieces from pale purple felt and eight nails from mint felt.

3. Glue or pin one palm pad piece and four toe pad pieces in position onto one of the paw pieces and sew in place **(b)**. If gluing, only use a very small amount of glue and wait for it to dry completely before sewing.

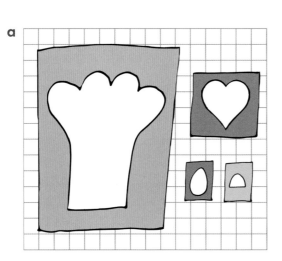

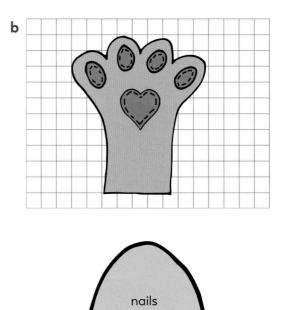

nails

4. With the front side of the paw facing downwards, place the elastic over the wrist end of the paw and fold the felt over the top. Sew across the top of the fold to secure in place and trim any excess felt above the sewn line if necessary. Glue a turquoise nail onto the back of each 'finger' so that it extends a little beyond the tip as shown **(c)**.

c

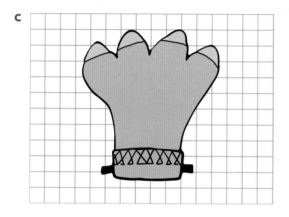

5. Place a piece of pink felt that is slightly larger than the paw onto a piece of pink felt that is the same size or larger than it. Place the paw, right side facing up, on top of the two pieces of felt and sew around the edges of the paw, leaving the wrist end and one side of the elastic open, as shown by the 'X' on the diagram **(d)**.

d

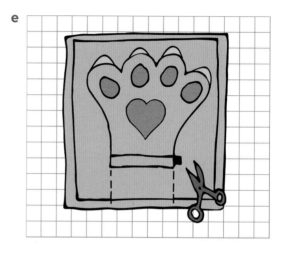 style placement

6. Trim away any excess felt around the edges of the paw without trimming around the wrist opening **(e)**.

e

7. Lightly stuff the paw between the two back layers of felt and then sew these two layers of felt together.

8. Slightly pull the elastic to create a cinched effect at the wrist before sewing above the elastic. Trim away any excess felt around the wrist opening **(f)**.

f

9. Repeat steps 3–8 to create a second paw.

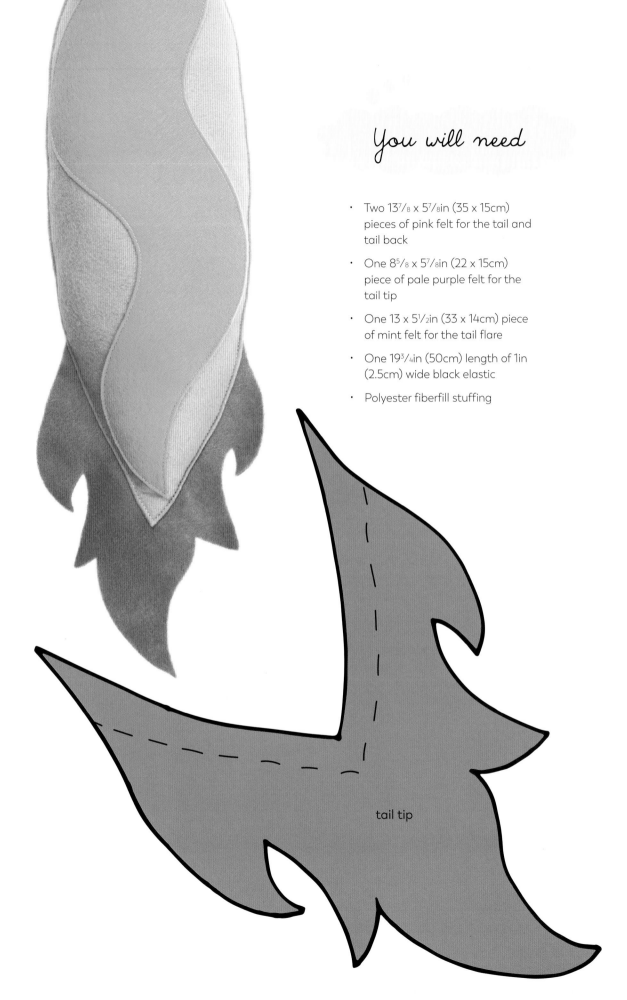

You will need

- Two 13⅞ x 5⅞in (35 x 15cm) pieces of pink felt for the tail and tail back
- One 8⅝ x 5⅞in (22 x 15cm) piece of pale purple felt for the tail tip
- One 13 x 5½in (33 x 14cm) piece of mint felt for the tail flare
- One 19¾in (50cm) length of 1in (2.5cm) wide black elastic
- Polyester fiberfill stuffing

tail tip

1. Copy the template for the tail, the unicorn tail flare (see Templates) and tail tip onto paper and then cut them out.

2. Pin all the paper templates to your selected felt colors and carefully cut them out **(a)**. Cut the tail from pink felt, the tail flare from mint felt and the tail tip from pale purple felt.

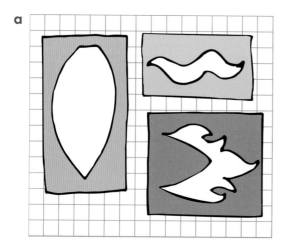

a

3. Pin or glue the tail flare piece to the tail. If gluing, wait until it is completely dry. Sew the piece in place **(b)**.

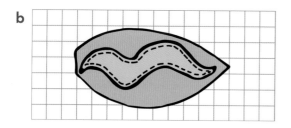

b

4. Layer the unicorn tail over the tail tip as shown. Place on a rectangle of pink felt (the backing rectangle needs to be slightly larger than the tail itself) **(c)**.

c

5. Sew all the pieces together following the outline of the basic pink tail piece, and leaving an opening at the straight end for stuffing. Trim the excess from the bottom rectangle to match the shape of the basic tail. Do not trim the tail tip!

6. Lightly stuff the tail, then turn it on its side, pinch the opening and insert both ends of the elastic. Pin in place and sew across the opening to secure the elastic in position **(d)**.

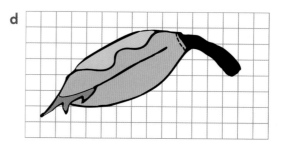

d

BRAVE LIKE A DRAGON

Dragons have a bad reputation for breathing fire to protect their hoard of gold, but dragons aren't ALL bad! They are also a symbol of strength, good luck, energy and ambition. It takes a lot of bravery and integrity to be the unpopular protector of treasures while knights are constantly poking you with shiny sticks: sometimes the most hated creatures are also the bravest creatures of all!

You will need

- Two 7 x 6³/₄in (18 x 17cm) pieces of green felt for the mask

- Two 7⁷/₈ x 4³/₈in (20 x 11cm) pieces and two ⁵/₈ x ³/₄in (1.5 x 2cm) pieces of black felt for the horns and nostrils

- One 4¹/₂ x 2³/₄in (11.5 x 7cm) piece and two 5⁷/₈ x 3in (15 x 7.5cm) pieces of tan felt for the snout and mask wings

- One 13in (33cm) length of ³/₈in (1cm) wide black elastic

1. Copy the mythical creature mask, dragon horns, dragon mask wing templates (see Templates), and the snout and nostril templates onto paper and cut out.

2. Cut the ears from the mask template and pin the paper templates onto felt in your chosen colors **(a)**. Cut one mask piece from green felt (including the eye holes), one snout piece from tan felt, one horns piece from black felt, two mask wing pieces from tan felt and two nostril pieces from black felt.

a

3. Place the felt horns onto a piece of black felt that is slightly larger than the horns. Pin in place, sew around the edges of the horns and trim all the way around the horns and set them aside. Glue or pin the nostrils to the snout and sew in place. Glue or pin the snout to the mask and sew in place **(b)**.

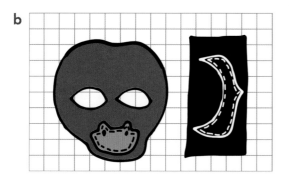

b

4. Place the felt dragon mask onto a piece of green felt slightly larger than the mask itself; pin in place. Place the felt mask wings between the felt mask piece and the back piece on each side of the mask as shown, and pin in place. Pin the elastic in place on either side of the mask between the two layers of felt (marked with 'X's); sew around the edges of the mask to attach the felt layers together **(c)**. Ensure the elastic is not twisted as you sew it in place on each side.

c

5. Pin the horns to the top of the dragon mask, and sew across the middle as shown to secure in place **(d)**.

d

6. Trim away any excess felt around the edges of the mask, carefully cutting the felt behind the wings and horn and inside the eye holes **(e)**.

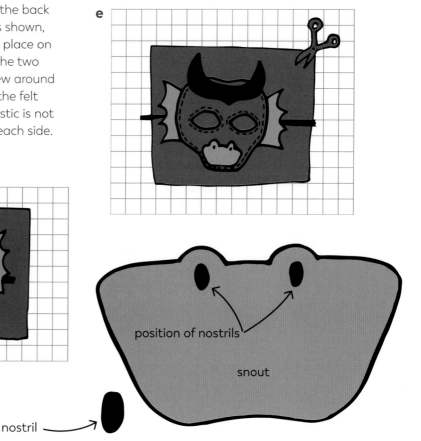

e

position of nostrils

snout

nostril

You will need

- Four 9½ x 10⅝in (24 x 27cm) pieces of green felt for the paws

- Two 9½ x 10⅝in (24 x 27cm) pieces of black felt for the paw interiors

- Two 3½ x 4in (9 x 10cm) pieces and eight 2⅛ x 2½in (5.5 x 6.5cm) pieces of tan felt for the palm and toe pads

- Two 5½in (14cm) lengths of ⅜in (1cm) wide black elastic

- Polyester fiberfill stuffing

1. Copy the paw, palm pad and toe pad templates (see Templates) onto paper and cut out.

2. Pin the paper templates onto felt in your chosen colors **(a)**. Cut two paw pieces from green felt, two palm pad pieces from tan felt and eight toe pad pieces from tan felt.

3. Glue or pin one palm pad piece and four toe pad pieces in position onto one of the paw pieces and sew in place **(b)**. If gluing, only use a very small amount of glue and wait for it to dry completely before sewing.

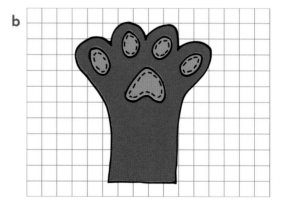

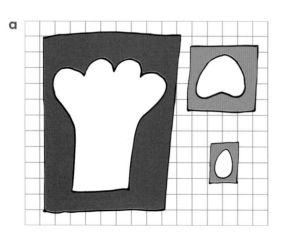

4. With the front side of the paw facing downwards, place the elastic over the wrist end of the paw and fold the felt over the top. Sew across the top of the fold to secure in place and trim any excess felt above the sewn line if necessary **(c)**.

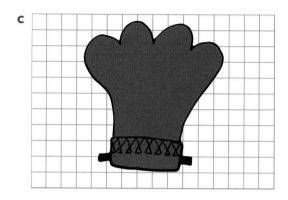

5. Place a piece of black felt that is slightly larger than the paw onto a piece of green felt that is the same size or larger than the black piece. Place the paw on top of the two pieces of felt and sew around the edges of the paw, leaving the wrist end and one side of the elastic open, as shown by the 'X' **(d)**.

6. Trim away any excess felt around the edges of the paw without trimming around the wrist opening **(e)**.

7. Lightly stuff the paw between the two back layers of felt and then sew these two layers of felt together.

8. Slightly pull the elastic to create a cinched effect at the wrist before sewing over the elastic. Trim away any excess felt around the wrist opening **(f)**.

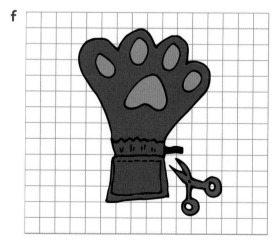

9. Repeat steps 3–8 to create a second paw.

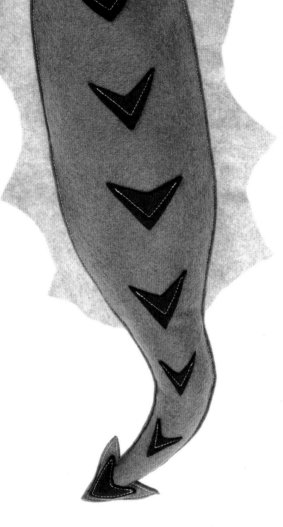

You will need

- Two 17³/₄ x 5⁷/₈in (45 x 15cm) pieces of green felt for the tail and tail back
- Seven 1³/₄ x 1³/₄in (4.5 x 4.5cm) pieces of black felt for the tail accents
- Two 35 x 12cm (13⁷/₈ x 4³/₄in) pieces of tan felt for the tail wings
- One 19³/₄in (50cm) length of 1in (2.5cm) wide black elastic
- Polyester fiberfill stuffing

1. Copy the tail and dragon tail wing (see Templates), and the tail tip and tail accent templates onto paper and cut them out.

2. Pin the paper templates onto felt in your chosen colors, aligning then attaching the dragon tail tip paper template to the dragon tail paper template as shown by the dotted line on the tail tip template. Cut one dragon tail piece from green felt, two tail wing pieces from tan felt and seven tail accent pieces from black felt **(a)**.

3. Trim the accent pieces to slightly different shapes if you wish (see photograph of tail). Glue or pin the tail accent pieces in position on the tail and sew in place **(b)**. If gluing, only use a very small amount of glue and wait for it to dry completely before sewing.

b

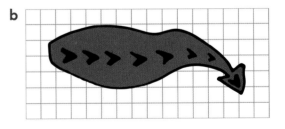

a

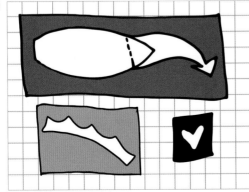

4. Place the felt dragon tail onto a piece of green felt that is slightly larger than the tail itself and pin in place. Place the felt dragon wings between the felt tail piece and the back piece on each side of the tail as shown, and pin in place. Sew around the edges of the tail, leaving the straight end open **(c)**.

6. Lightly stuff the tail. Turn the tail on its side, pinch the opening and insert both ends of the elastic. Pin in place and sew across the opening to secure in place **(e)**.

e
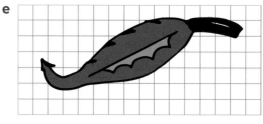

c
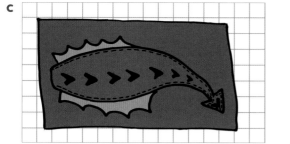

5. Trim away any excess felt around the edges of the tail without trimming around the opening, carefully cutting the tail behind the wings **(d)**.

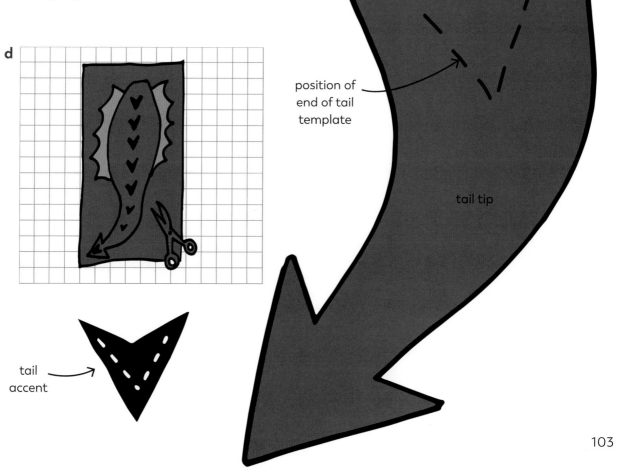

position of end of tail template

tail tip

d

tail accent

MISCHIEVOUS LIKE A MONSTER

We all need a little mischief every now and then. This little monster is sure to find all sorts of tricky business to get into. This monster costume can be made in absolutely any color combination to suit your little monster's spirit perfectly. Dressing up as a monster could be a great way to giggle the grumpies out or to play a trick on your grandparents!

MONSTER MASK

You will need

- Two 7½ x 7in (19 x 18cm) pieces, four 3½ x 2⅜in (9 x 6cm) pieces and one 5⅛ x 2⅜in (13 x 6cm) piece of blue felt for the mask, ears and chin

- Three 2½ x 2in (6.5 x 5cm) pieces of gold felt for the eyebrows and hair

- Four 4 x 2½in (10 x 6.5cm) pieces and two 1⅜ x 1¾in (3.5 x 4.5cm) pieces of cream felt for the horns and teeth

- One 13in (33cm) length of ⅜in (1cm) wide black elastic

1. Copy the mythical creature mask and monster horn (see Templates), chin, hair, ear, eyebrow and tooth templates onto paper and cut out.

2. Cut the ears off the mask template and pin the paper templates onto felt in your chosen colors **(a)**. Cut one mask piece (including the eye holes), one chin piece and two monster ear pieces from blue felt, one hair piece and two eyebrow pieces from gold felt, and two tooth pieces and two horn pieces from cream felt.

a

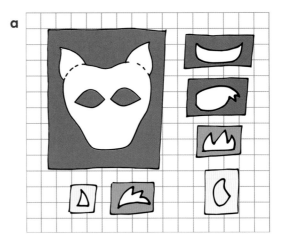

3. Glue or pin the eyebrows and teeth to the mask and sew in place as shown. Place the felt horns onto a piece of cream felt that is slightly larger than them, and the felt ears onto a piece of blue felt, again slightly larger them **(b)**. Pin in place, sew around the edges of the horns and the ears and trim away the excess felt.

c

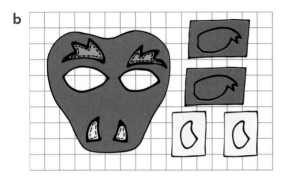

b

5. Trim away any excess felt around the edges of the mask, carefully cutting the felt behind the ears, horns and hair, and inside the eye holes.

4. Place the monster mask onto a rectangle of blue felt that is larger than the mask, then pin and sew the chin in position. Place the felt ears, horns and hair between the felt mask piece and the backing rectangle as shown, and pin in place. Pin the mask and the backing together with the elastic in place on one side of the mask (marked by an 'X'), between the layers. Sew around the edges to attach the two pieces of felt together. Ensure that your elastic is not twisted as you slide the other end of it in between the layers when you get to that point on the mask, as shown by the other 'X' **(c)**.

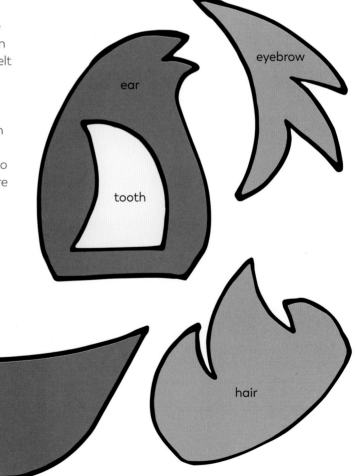

ear

eyebrow

tooth

chin

hair

You will need

- Six 9¹⁄₂ x 10⁵⁄₈in (24 x 27cm) pieces of blue felt for the paws and paw interiors

- Two 3¹⁄₂ x 4in (9 x 10cm) pieces and eight 2¹⁄₈ x 2¹⁄₂in (5.5 x 6.5cm) pieces of gold felt for the palm and toe pads

- Two 5¹⁄₂in (14cm) lengths of ³⁄₈in (1cm) wide black elastic

- Polyester fiberfill stuffing

1. Copy the paw, palm pad and toe pad templates (see Templates) onto paper and cut out.

2. Pin the paper templates onto felt in your chosen colors **(a)**. Cut two paw pieces from blue felt, two palm pad pieces from gold felt and eight toe pad pieces from gold felt.

3. Glue or pin one palm pad piece and four toe pad pieces in position onto one of the paw pieces and sew in place **(b)**. If gluing, only use a very small amount of glue and wait for it to dry completely before sewing.

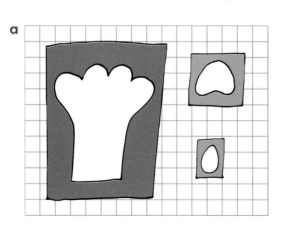

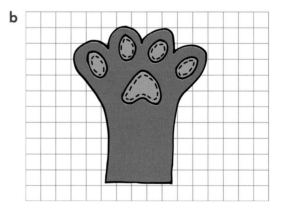

4. With the front side of the paw facing downwards, place the elastic over the wrist end of the paw and fold the felt over the top. Sew across the top of the fold to secure in place and trim any excess felt above the sewn line if necessary **(c)**.

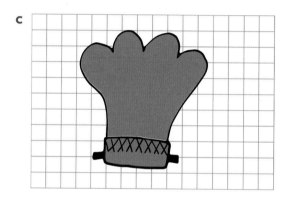

c

5. Place a piece of blue felt that is slightly larger than the paw onto a piece of blue felt that is the same size or larger than it. Place the paw on top of the two pieces of felt and sew around the edges of the paw, leaving one side of the elastic and the wrist end open, as shown by the 'X' **(d)**.

d

6. Trim away any excess felt around the edges of the paw without trimming around the wrist opening **(e)**.

e

7. Lightly stuff the paw between the two back layers of felt and then sew these two layers of felt together.

8. Slightly pull the elastic to create a cinched effect at the wrist before sewing over the elastic. Trim away any excess felt around the wrist opening **(f)**.

f

9. Repeat steps 3–8 to create a second paw.

You will need

- Two 13⅞ x 5⅞in (35 x 15cm) pieces of blue felt for the tail and tail back
- Two 5½ x 4in (14 x 10cm) pieces of gold felt for the stripes
- Six 4 x 2⅜in (10 x 6cm) pieces of cream felt for the spikes
- One 19¾in (50cm) length of 1in (2.5cm) wide black elastic
- Polyester fiberfill stuffing

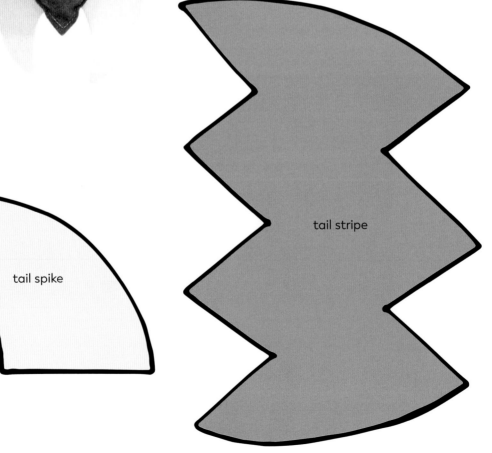

tail stripe

tail spike

1. Copy the tail (see Templates), the tail spike and the tail stripe templates onto paper and cut out.

2. Pin the paper templates onto felt in your chosen colors **(a)**. Cut one tail piece from blue felt, two tail stripe pieces from gold felt and six tail spike pieces from cream felt.

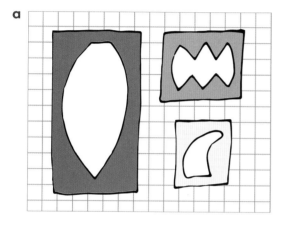

3. Glue or pin the tail stripe pieces in position on the tail and sew in place **(b)**. If gluing, only use a very small amount of glue and wait for it to dry completely before sewing.

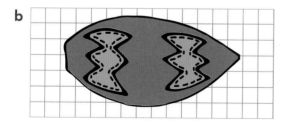

4. Place the felt monster tail onto a piece of blue felt that is slightly larger than the tail itself. Place the felt tail spikes between the tail piece and the back piece on each side of the tail as shown, and pin in place. Sew around the edges of the tail, leaving the straight end open. Trim away any excess felt around the tail without trimming around the opening, and carefully cutting the tail behind the spikes **(c)**.

5. Lightly stuff the tail. Turn the tail on its side, pinch the opening and insert both ends of the elastic. Pin in place and sew across the opening to secure in place **(d)**.

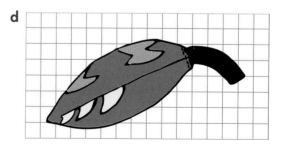

All templates in this section and throughout the book are shown at actual size. You can download printable versions of these templates from: http://ideas.sewandso.co.uk/patterns.

Wild animal mask

Bird mask

Owl head feathers

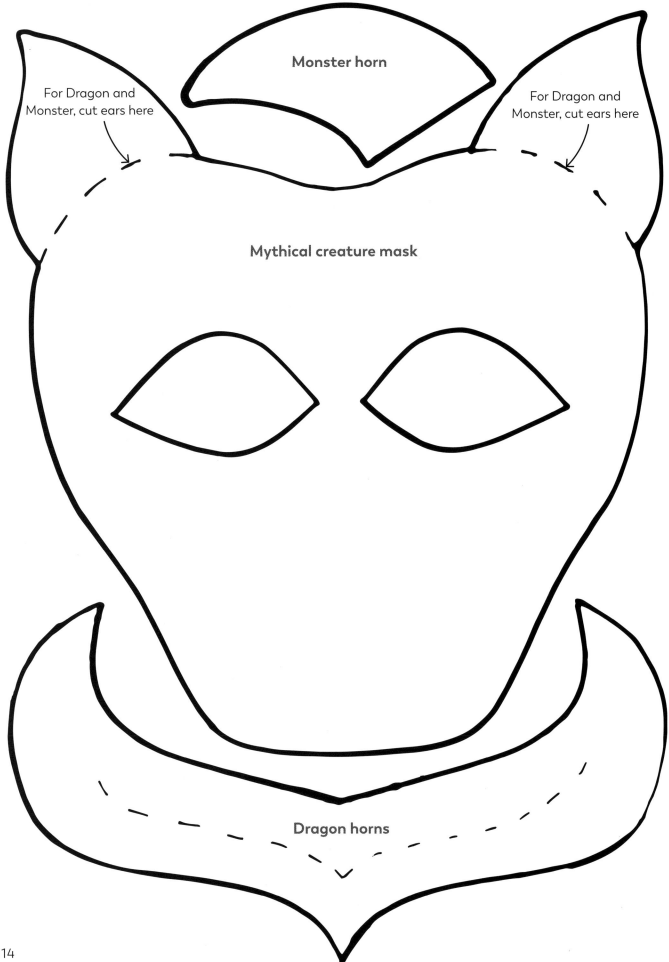

Monster horn

For Dragon and Monster, cut ears here

For Dragon and Monster, cut ears here

Mythical creature mask

Dragon horns

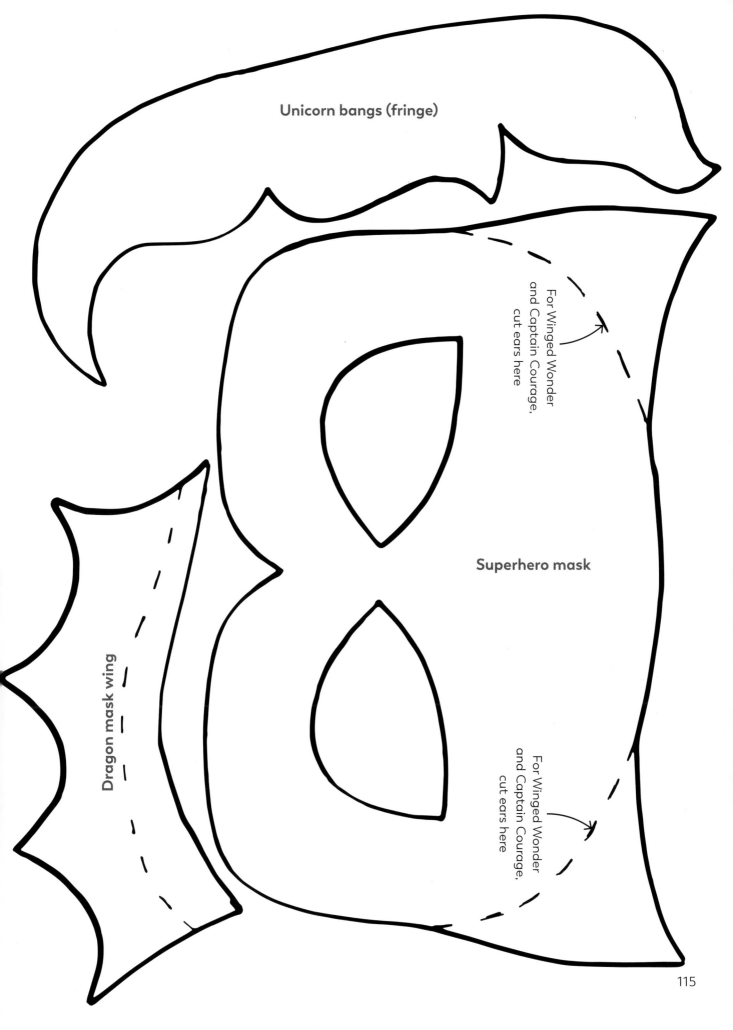

Unicorn bangs (fringe)

For Winged Wonder and Captain Courage, cut ears here

Superhero mask

Dragon mask wing

For Winged Wonder and Captain Courage, cut ears here

115

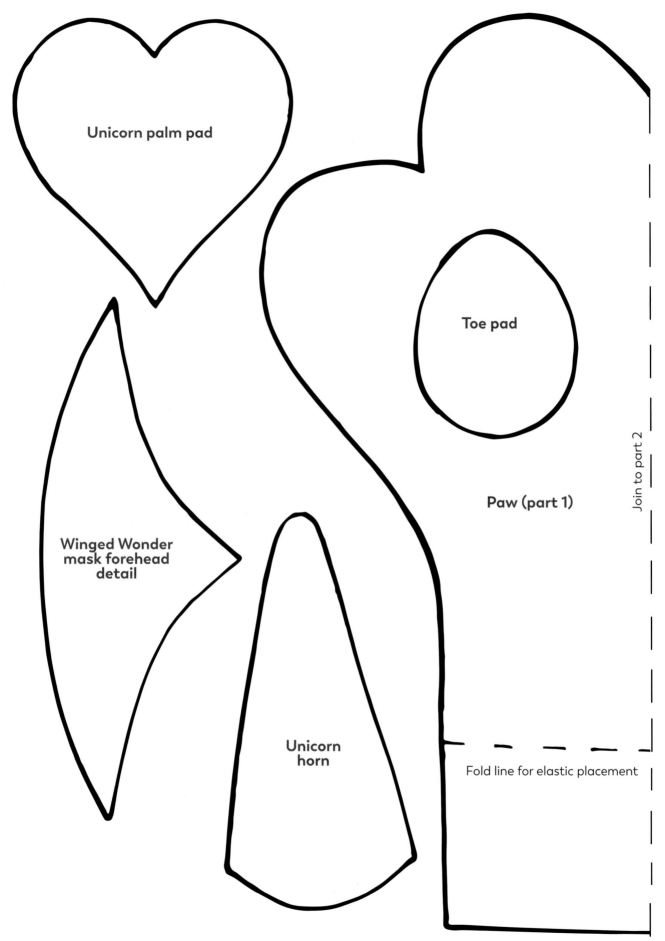

Unicorn palm pad

Toe pad

Paw (part 1)

Join to part 2

Winged Wonder mask forehead detail

Unicorn horn

Fold line for elastic placement

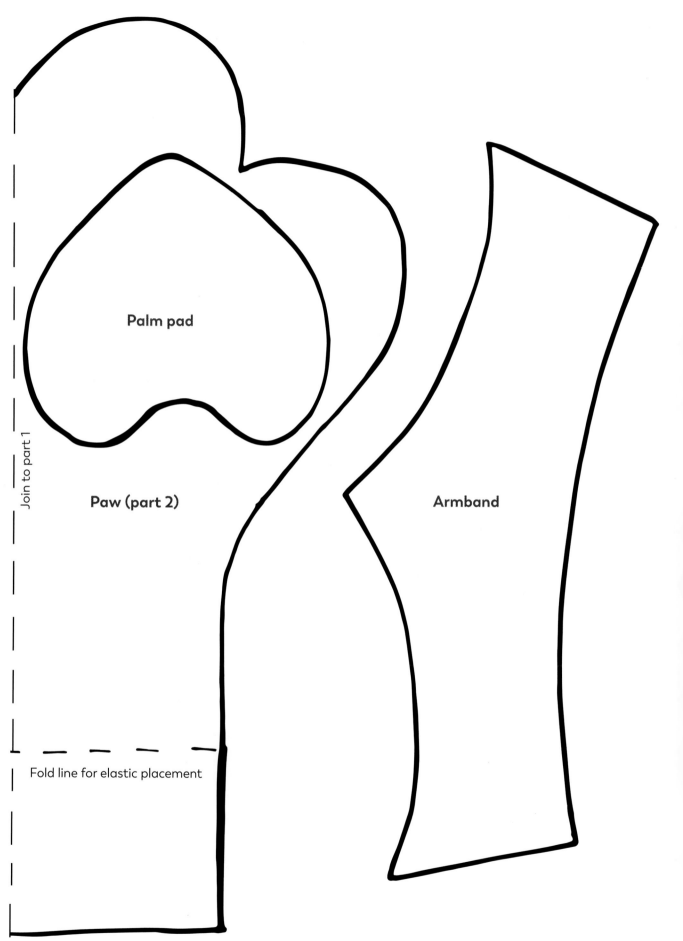

Palm pad

Paw (part 2)

Join to part 1

Fold line for elastic placement

Armband

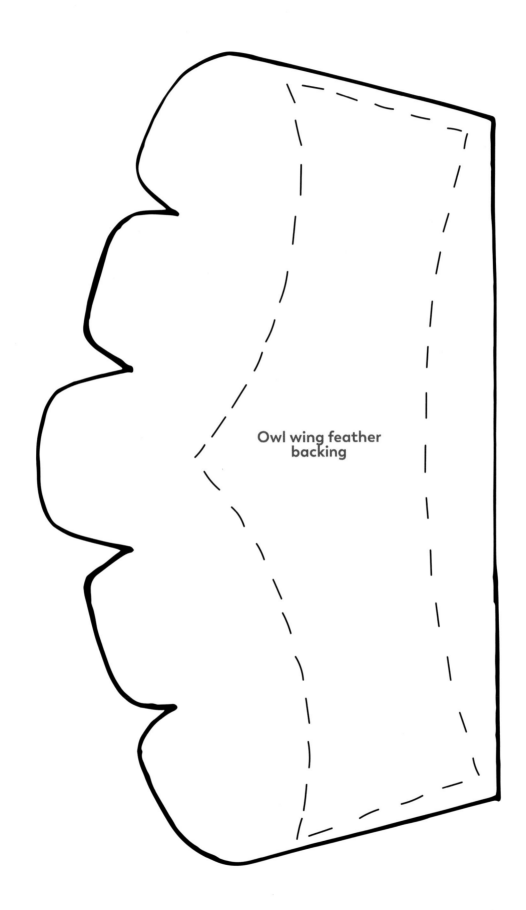

Owl wing feather
backing

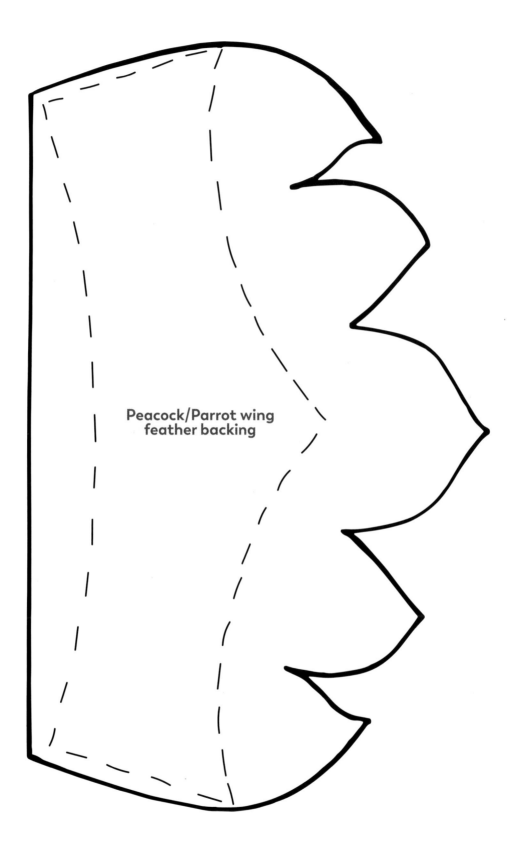

Peacock/Parrot wing
feather backing

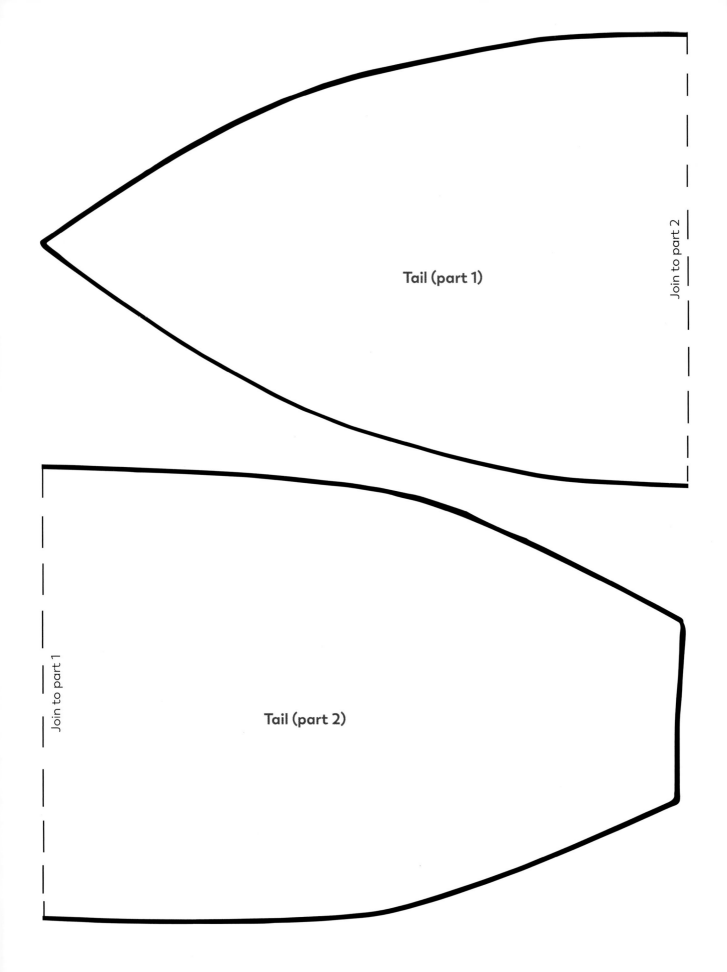

Tail (part 1)

Join to part 2

Join to part 1

Tail (part 2)

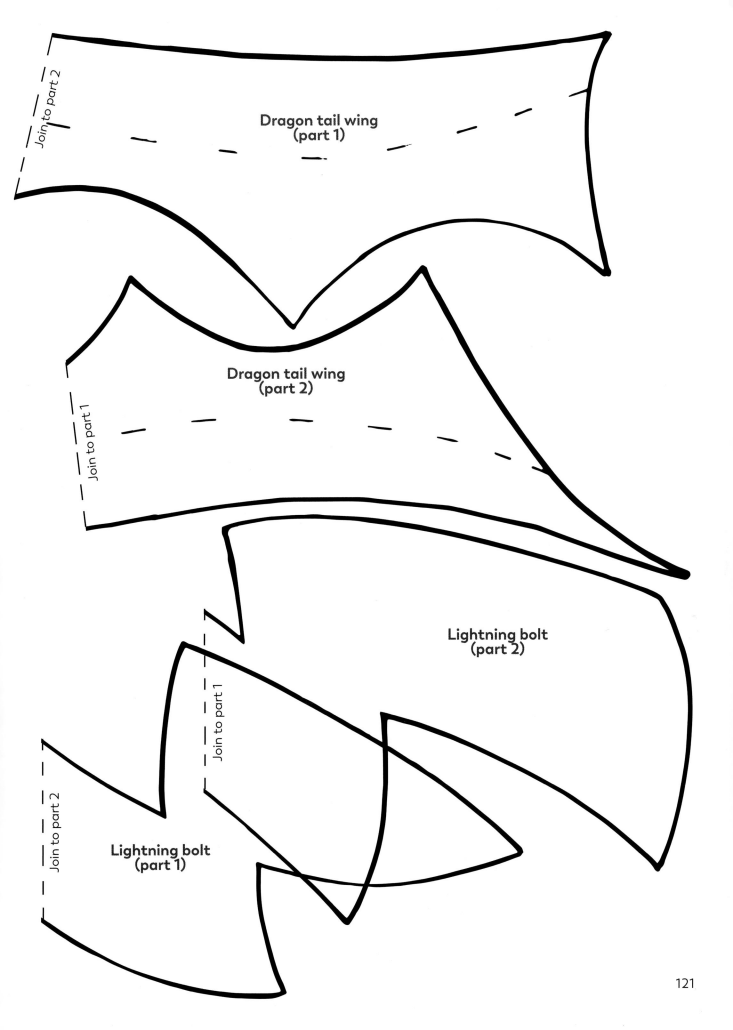

Dragon tail wing
(part 1)

Join to part 2

Dragon tail wing
(part 2)

Join to part 1

Lightning bolt
(part 2)

Join to part 1

Join to part 2

Lightning bolt
(part 1)

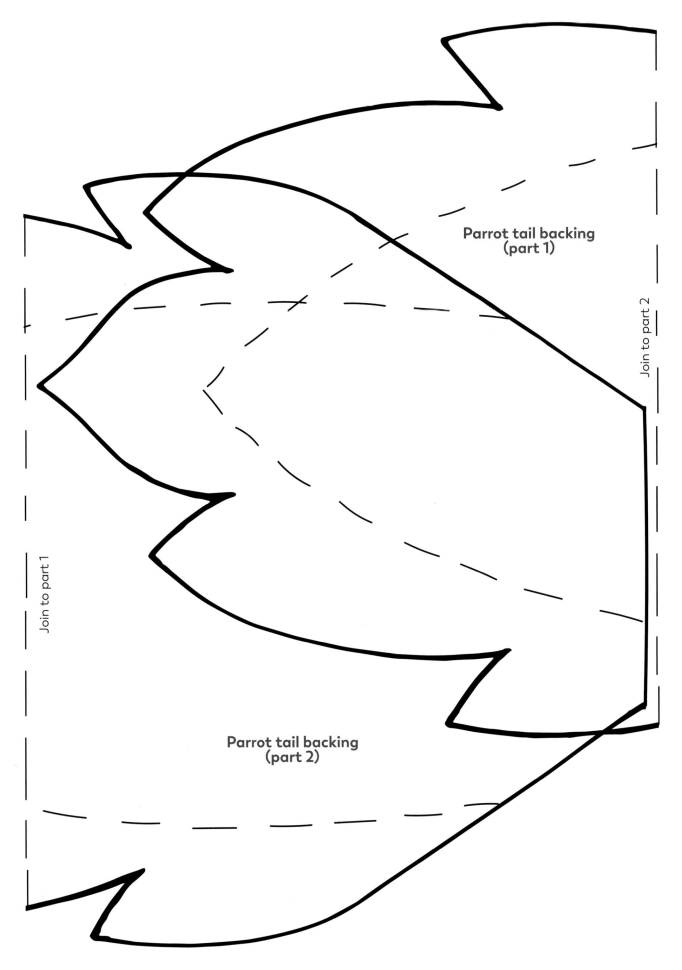

Parrot tail backing
(part 1)

Join to part 2

Join to part 1

Parrot tail backing
(part 2)

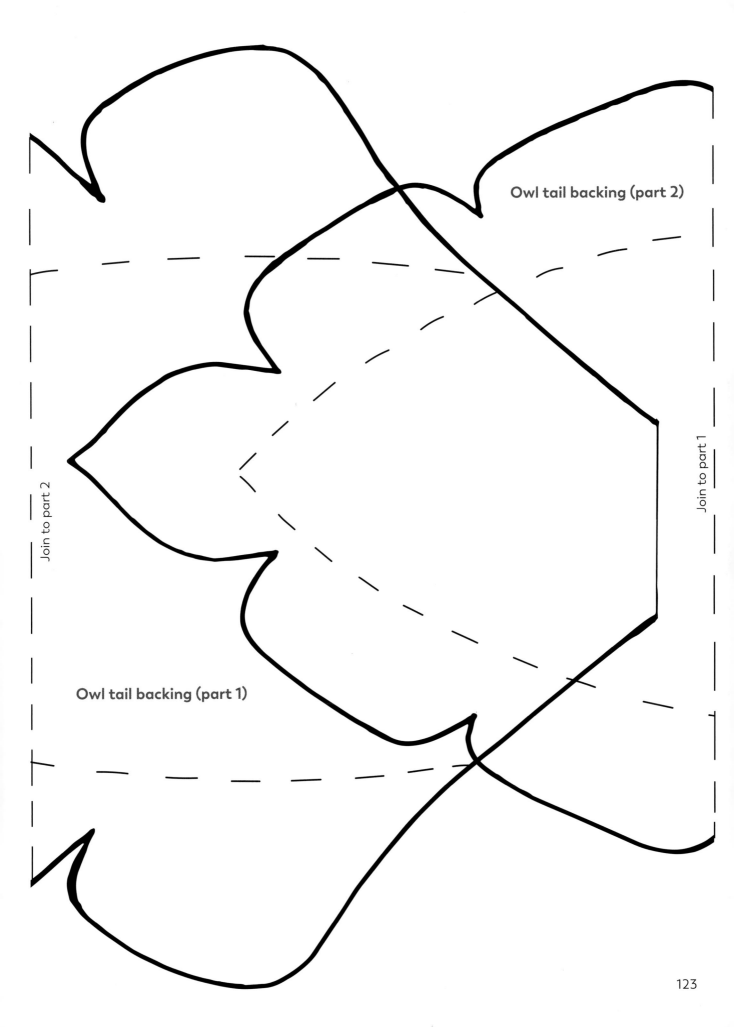

Owl tail backing (part 2)

Owl tail backing (part 1)

Join to part 2

Join to part 1

123

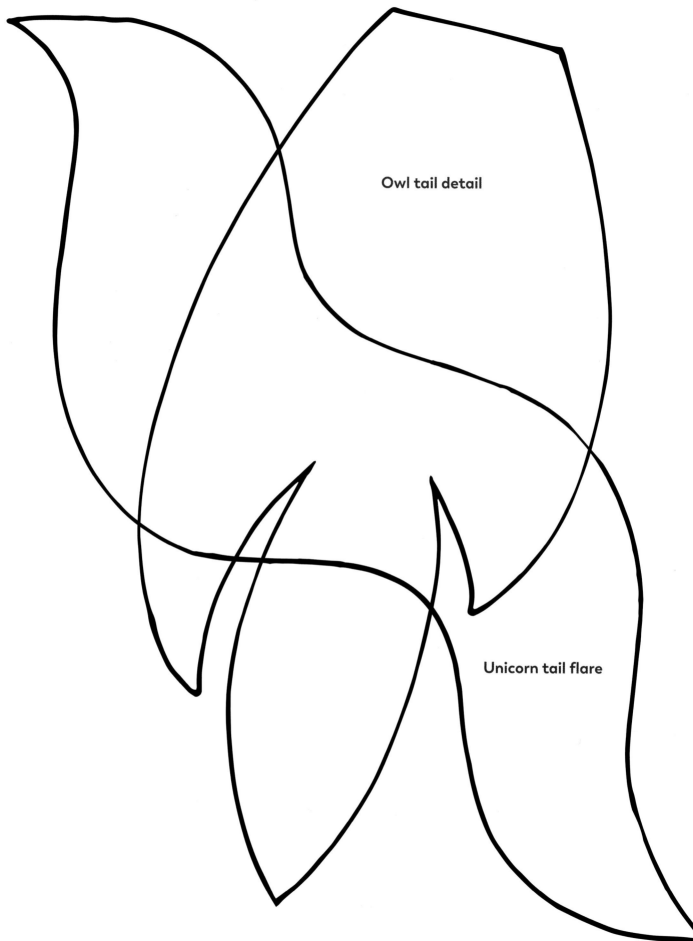

Owl tail detail

Unicorn tail flare

ABOUT THE AUTHOR

Jessica Near has been making felt costume pieces for children for over seven years for her business Opposite of Far, with the goal of promoting play and imagination for all children, young and older! Creating hundreds of original designs for animal masks, tails, ear headbands, paws and more, she has built quite a reputation for providing simple and high quality costume pieces that can be used day to day, year after year. Before starting her creative business, Jessica worked as a preschool teacher and nanny for many years. Her background is in Early Childhood Development and Education so everything she offers has a very thoughtful approach and a focus on learning through play.

SUPPLIERS

For more felt costume pieces made by Jessica Near, please visit the Opposite of Far website at www.oppositeoffar.com, or follow her on Instagram @oppositeoffar to shop and find out lots of animal facts and fun.

FELT

UK

SewandSo
www.sewandso.co.uk

US

Benzie Design
www.benziedesign.com

Kunin Premium Felt (Eco-fi Felt)
www.kuningroup.com/felt-collections/eco-fi-plus/

SCISSORS

Gingher
www.gingher.com

ELASTIC + OTHER NOTIONS

CTS USA
www.ctsusa.com

SEWING MACHINE

Bernina
www.bernina.com

STUFFING

Amazon, search for Poly-fil stuffing
www.amazon.com
www.amazon.co.uk

Acknowledgments

This book is dedicated to ALL my people. My friends, family, fellow makers and all the children who color this world with their boundless imaginations! I would like to thank the models in the book: Charlie, Evie, Fenn, Harper, LayLa, Lundin, May, Siri, Tevin, Will, and Primary (www.primary.com) and June and January (www.juneandjanuary.com) who very kindly supplied the clothing for our little models to wear. Thank you to everyone who has helped, inspired, collaborated, lifted, believed, encouraged and even discouraged me.

INDEX

A SEWANDSO BOOK
© F&W Media International, Ltd 2018

SewandSo is an imprint of F&W Media International, Ltd
Pynes Hill Court, Pynes Hill, Exeter, EX2 5AZ, UK

F&W Media International, Ltd is a subsidiary of F+W Media, Inc
10151 Carver Road, Suite #200, Blue Ash, OH 45242, USA

Text and Designs © Jessica Near 2018
Layout and Photography © F&W Media International, Ltd 2018

First published in the UK and USA in 2018

A catalogue record for this book is available from the British Library.

ISBN-13: 978-1-4463-0677-2 paperback
SRN: R6959 paperback

ISBN-13: 978-1-4463-7651-5 PDF
SRN: R7613 PDF

ISBN-13: 978-1-4463-7652-2 EPUB
SRN: R7612 EPUB

Printed in China by RR Donnelley for:
F&W Media International, Ltd
Pynes Hill Court, Pynes Hill, Exeter, EX2 5AZ, UK

10 9 8 7 6 5 4 3 2

Content Director: Ame Verso
Acquisitions Editor: Sarah Callard
Managing Editor: Jeni Hennah
Project Editor: Jane Trollope
Proofreader: Cheryl Brown
Design Manager: Lorraine Inglis
Designer: Ali Stark
Photographers: Qiana Kelsh and Jason Jenkins
Production Manager: Beverley Richardson

F&W Media publishes high quality books on a wide range of subjects.
For more great book ideas visit: www.sewandso.co.uk

Layout of the digital edition of this book may vary depending on reader hardware and display settings.